Consuming Cultu

CONTENTS

Feminist Review is published three times a year. It is edited by a Collective which is supported by a group of Corresponding Editors.

The Collective: Avtar Brah, Ann Phoenix, Annie Whitehead, Catherine Hall, Dot Griffiths, Gail Lewis, Helen Crowley, Merl Storr.

Corresponding Editors: Ailbhe Smyth, Ann Curthoys, Hala Shukrallah, Kum-Kum Bhavnani, Jacqui Alexander, Lidia Curti, Meera Kosambi, Patricia Mohammed, Sue O'Sullivan, Zarina Maharaj.

Correspondence and advertising
Contributions, books for review and editorial correspondence should be sent to: Feminist Review, 52 Featherstone Street, London EC1Y 8RT.
For advertising please write to:
Journals Advertising, Routledge, 11 New Fetter Lane, London EC4P 4EE, UK.
Tel: 0171 583 9855

Subscriptions
Please contact Routledge Subscriptions Department, Cheriton House, North Way, Andover, Hants SP10 5BE, UK. Tel: 44 (0)1264 342713; Fax 44 (0)1264 342807; for sample copy requests, e-mail sample.journals@routledge.com; for subscription and general information, e-mail info.journals@routledge.com. A full listing of Routledge books and journals is available by accessing http://www.routledge.com/routledge.html

Notes for Contributors
Authors should submit four copies of their work to: *Feminist Review*, 52 Featherstone Street, London, EC1Y 8RT. We assume that you will keep a copy of your work. Submission of work to *Feminist Review* will be taken to imply that it is original, unpublished work, which is not under consideration for publication elsewhere. All work is subject to a system of anonymous peer review. All work is refereed by at least two external (non-Collective) referees.

Please note that we cannot accept unsolicited book reviews.

Bookshop distribution in the USA
Routledge, 29 West 35th Street, New York, NY10001, USA.

Typeset by Type Study, Scarborough
Printed in Great Britain
by Bell & Bain Ltd, Glasgow

ISSN 0141-7789

The *Feminist Review* office has moved.
Please send all correspondence to:
Feminist Review
52 Featherstone Street
London EC1Y 8RT

Feminist Review was founded in 1979. Since that time it has established itself as one of the UK's leading feminist journals.

• Why not subscribe?
Make sure of your copy

All subscriptions run in calendar years. The issues for 1997 are Nos. 55, 56 and 57.

• Subscription rates, 1997 (3 issues)

Individual Subscriptions

UK/EEC	£29
Overseas	£29
North America	£46

A number of reduced cost (£20 per year: UK only) subscriptions are available for readers experiencing financial hardship, e.g. unemployed, student, low-paid. If you'd like to be considered for a reduced subscription, please write to the Collective, c/o the Feminist Review office, 52 Featherstone Street, London EC1Y 8RT.

Institutional Subscriptions

UK	£80	**Single Issues**	**£9.99**
Overseas	£88		
North America	$126		

☐ Please send me one year's subscription to **Feminist Review**

☐ Please send me _____ copies of back issue no. _____

METHOD OF PAYMENT

☐ I enclose a cheque/international money order to the value of _____
made payable to Routledge Journals

☐ Please charge my Access/Visa/American Express/Diners Club account

Account no. ☐☐☐☐☐☐☐☐☐☐☐☐☐☐☐☐☐☐

Expiry date _____   Signature _____

If the address below is different from the registered address of your credit card, please give your registered address separately.

PLEASE USE BLOCK CAPITALS

Name _____

Address _____

_____

_____

_____

_____ Postcode_____

☐ Please send me a Routledge Journals Catalogue

☐ Please send me a Routledge Gender and Women's Studies Catalogue

Please return this form with payment to:

Routledge Subscriptions Department, Cheriton House, North Way, Andover, Hants SP10 5BE

Editorial:

Consuming Cultures

This Special Issue of *Feminist Review* on **Consuming Cultures** is concerned with the interrelationship of gender and the circuits of consumption, distribution, production and reproduction. While there is an extensive body of work which focuses on gender and consumption or on gender and production, there is little which considers the different ways in which gender intervenes in all parts of the circuit or the linkages between the different elements. The Special Issue aims to make a contribution to the reframing of these debates.

These complex relationships operate simultaneously on different sites both local and global, which are always played out in relations of power. Consuming cultures are thus gendered, racialized, sexualized and intersected by relations of social class. The Special Issue is concerned with the ways in which the local and the global are implicated in each other and how gender is played out in each. How, for example, do changes in one part of that relation (local–global) impact on the other part? How do such changes and the power relations they constitute affect the production of gendered identities in all the sites of the circuit? What part do pleasure and desire play in the production of these identities? How do people become commodified in the process of production and consumption and what are the different contexts in which people may be active in their own commodification? The articles in this issue address these questions in various ways and from a range of disciplines.

Chris Griffin examines the centrality of consumption in the normative assessment of young people's successful transition to adulthood. Often, young people who are identified as failing are seen to do so in terms of their non-conformity to particular patterns of consumption. The ideals of consumption against which young people are measured generally assume 'youth' to be a unitary category. This fails to take account of the ways in which youth are differentiated by gender, class, 'race' and of the ways in which young people's habits of consumption vary. Griffin's paper reminds us that consumption can simultaneously be used as a regulatory device and, contradictorily, as part of young people's own practices of identification.

FEMINIST REVIEW NO 55, SPRING 1997, pp. 1–3

The ways in which consumption both produces regimes of knowledge about us and is used by us in the production of our own identifications is discussed by Donna Haraway in her analysis of the impact of new reproductive technologies. She interrogates the representation of 'creation' as a way of discussing the debates around biotechnologies of reproduction, looking at images as diverse as Michelangelo's 'Creation' and the sonogram imaging of the fetus in the womb. Haraway explores the subjective impact and political ramifications of the many metaphors deployed by so-called objective science and other discursive cultural formations for describing and visualizing the changing boundaries of the female body. Her analysis of the political power of these metaphors enables debates about consumption to be linked to contentious debates surrounding reproductive freedom and 'overpopulation' and the ethical and moral considerations that these raise.

Both Griffin's and Haraway's papers foreground the contradictory nature of consumption: it is often experienced as a matter of individual (and, sometimes, oppositional) choice; at the same time it can also function as a method of surveillance and control. It is the possibilities of extracting pleasure from the consumption/production relation, even as one recognizes its potential for exploitation that is addressed, in different ways, by Reina Lewis and Angela McRobbie. McRobbie argues against recent celebrations of consumption in the human sciences by insisting that not everyone has equal access to the consumption of fashion. She examines the gendered and racialized relations of production in the fashion industry without resurrecting the unified subject of some previous class analyses. Her account of how women make and acquire their clothes inside and outside the fashion industry permits us to recognize that there is no necessary contradiction between being an exploited worker in the fashion industry and desiring its products. McRobbie's paper raises questions about how it might be possible to organize for political change in the light of these personal investments.

While McRobbie focuses on the production and consumption of garments, Reina Lewis looks at how the consumption of fashion imagery is itself pleasurable and constitutive of identity. She examines the complexities of the 'identification as consumption' model celebrated by the new lesbian and gay lifestyle press which emerged in the context of the 'pink pound'. By focusing specifically on the fashion editorial content of lesbian lifestyle magazines, Lewis engages with questions about the lesbian and the female gaze. She discusses how pleasures obtained in the transgressive consumption of 'mainstream' women's fashion magazines disappear when lesbian pleasure becomes the overt remit of the lesbian lifestyle magazine.

Visual culture is also addressed in Annie Coombes' discussion with the South African artist, Penny Siopis. Coombes' paper illustrates the ideological nature of visual imagery. Along with other radical South African artists, feminist artists are currently debating questions of priority now that Liberation has arrived. For feminists, this is potentially a very positive moment when questions of gender – so long subordinated to the structural issue of race under apartheid – can now be explored. Penny Siopis' work has long been concerned with the lived and historical relations between black and white women in South Africa and the appropriation of black women's time, lives and labour at different historical conjunctures. This discussion reminds us that culture is never innocently produced or consumed, but is always situated in specific historical and geographical locations and power relations.

Joanna de Groot situates the restructuring of the British system of higher education in its historical context in order to explore how, as subjects, academics are being reconstructed. She argues that one key way to understand these material and cultural transformations is to think of them as processes of commodification: of academic labour, skills and intellectual production. De Groot focuses on the gender dynamics of both the process and the experience of shifting norms, values and practices within academia.

From their different disciplinary perspectives, all the papers in this issue consider the contradictory nature of subjectivities and desire in relation to consumption and production. They illustrate how patterns of consumption are changing. Not only can we talk about the consumption of culture/s but also how the obsession with the act of consumption itself has transformed both the markets and the process of production. Not only do we consume culture/s but we are also consumed by them.

In opening up these questions, this issue of *Feminist Review* invites a rethinking of the production/distribution/consumption circuit in relation to the new regimes of accumulation, power and politics produced by late capitalism at the end of the millennium.

Avtar Brah
Annie E.Coombes
Reina Lewis
Ann Phoenix

Troubled Teens:

Managing Disorders of Transition and Consumption

Christine Griffin

FEMINIST REVIEW NO 55, SPRING 1997, pp. 4–21

Abstract

This article focuses on the representation of youth as a key moment of transition in contemporary western societies, set between the dependent state of childhood and the supposed maturity and independence of adult status. Young people are viewed as gendered, racialized and sexualized beings who also occupy specific class locations, and are assumed to move through crucial points of transition as they leave full-time education and enter the job market, as well as the (hetero)sexual and marriage marketplaces. The article examines some of the main discursive configurations and treatment regimes through which 'troubled teens' are constructed and managed, especially in relation to notions about disordered patterns of consumption and transition. The paper considers the moment of the 'discovery' of adolescence in the late nineteenth century, going on to examine young women's particular relationships to discourses around consumption in the contemporary British youth research literature, and to debates about 'disrupted transitions' and citizenship in the 1990s. The article ends with a brief examination of one approach to the 'problem of troubled teens' in the USA: Specialty Schools that offer a combination of educational, therapeutic and correctional regimes aimed at young people who have been identified in relation to various disorders of transition and consumption.

Keywords

youth; consumption; transition; citizenship; treatment; education; therapy; problem youth

In the summer of 1995 I spent two months in Southern California teaching Summer School. During my visit there was considerable (albeit brief) coverage in the local press and TV news of a young man who had died whilst on a type of 'therapeutic' outdoor camping expedition organized specifically for 'defiant teens'. This was not the only instance of death or serious injury that had occurred in 'wilderness programmes' organized by this particular company, and further investigation revealed a mass of similar 'packages' for young people, which were targeted carefully at particular groups of young women and men – or rather at their parents. The 'wilderness programmes' and 'individualized education plans' offered by

4

what are known as 'Specialty Schools' in the USA are concerned to police and smooth over potentially difficult moments of transition to adulthood in a 'caring' yet controlling way.

Young people occupy a distinct position in the circuit of consumption, distribution, production and reproduction, which is gendered, sexualized and located in class- and 'race'-specific contexts. In contemporary western societies, youth represents a key moment of transition between the dependent state of childhood and the supposed maturity and independence of adulthood. Young people are located at crucial points of transition as they leave full-time education, enter the job market, and enter the sexual (and marriage) markets (Griffin, 1982). For some the moment of leaving education occurs at 16, for others it is 18 or 22; many young people remain marginal to the job market, as unemployed or on government-sponsored training schemes; and some are marginal to the dominant (hetero)sexual and marriage markets through identifying as gay, lesbian or bisexual. Such 'variations' are not simply a matter of individual differences: these key transitions in the move to adult status construct an idealized norm of the 'right' way to grow up as an adolescent, in order to find your future place in the adult world.

In this article I want to examine some of the main discursive configurations and treatment regimes through which 'troubled teens' are constructed and managed. In particular, I want to develop arguments I have made elsewhere concerning the representation of young people themselves as potentially 'troubled' and subject to specific disorders of consumption and transition (Griffin, 1993). I will also consider the ways in which such representations of 'troubled teens' are gendered, racialized and class-specific. It has been most common to examine young people's location as consumers of material goods, including the construction of 'teenage' markets for music, clothes, make-up, cigarettes, alcohol and so on (Abrams, 1959; cf. Miles, 1995). I want to consider the construction of (certain) young people as *disordered* consumers in racially-structured patriarchal capitalist societies.

Although the primary focus of this paper appears to be youth, I would see this work as a feminist analysis. Many feminist approaches have taken analyses of gender (and also sexual) relations as their primary focus, along with an interest in and commitment to examining issues from women's perspective(s) (Richardson and Robinson, 1992; Griffin and Phoenix, 1994). This approach has predominated amongst Anglo-feminists of the 'First World', and it proved a valuable strategy in specific historical and political contexts (especially from the late 1960s onwards). By the 1990s, it has become more commonplace (though by no means universal) for feminists to argue that gender and/or sexuality can never be considered in isolation

from 'race', class or disability (Mohanty *et al.*, 1991). In addition, those influenced by post-structuralism and postmodernism would question the value of unitary terms such as 'woman' and 'gender' (see Tong, 1989, for brief review).

My approach is somewhat different since I would certainly argue that gender can never be considered in isolation, but in a given context relations of gender, sexuality, 'race', class and disability may (or may not) intersect in a variety of ways. I have been interested in deconstructing notions of 'youth' and 'adolescence', and I would want to retain that deconstructivist perspective with respect to 'gender', 'woman' and other major social categories. Unlike some feminists who have drawn on post-structuralist and postmodern perspectives, I would not deconstruct such categories out of existence. 'Youth', 'adolescence', 'gender', 'race' and so on *can* be deconstructed completely, but they each still retain an undeniable social, psychological, cultural and economic force in specific contexts, and I aim to work with the tension between these two positions. My focus on the nature of constructed transitions into the 'adult' cycle of production/reproduction/consumption for young people does not imply that gender, 'race', class, sexuality and disability are irrelevant or marginal: quite the contrary. I also wish to consider the possibility that in some contexts, gender (and sexuality, 'race' and/or class) may be absent, and that this absence might be worthy of analysis in itself.

Why should youth/adolescence represent such a key moment in contemporary western societies as far as the circuit of consumption/production/reproduction is concerned? The moment of 'youth' (which in practice is a complex series of intersecting moments) is above all about transition and change, and about the *management* of that change. Whilst the dominant model of adolescence, that of physiologically-driven Storm and Stress,

Specialty Schools

locates such change as biologically determined, many discourses around youth represent the necessity for the young person to learn self-control (e.g. Conger, 1979). The moment of (potentially dangerous) change and transition epitomized by 'youth' is important precisely because it operates in contrast to prevailing notions of innocent dependent childhood and static mature adult status. Constructions of the latter categories are reinforced by default through dominant representations of what it means to be young.

The century since the 'discovery' of adolescence by early US psychologist G. Stanley Hall has seen a series of moral panics over youth by adults in academia, government, social and welfare work (Hall, 1904; Muncie, 1984). The most recent manifestations of such panics include concerns over 'teenage pregnancy', rising youth crime, drug use (e.g. over ecstasy in the UK), and the apathetic 'slackers' of 'Generation X'. Such panics tend to focus on particular groups of young people. In the USA, the incidence of parenthood amongst young, single African-American women was identified as a key factor in the 1992 Los Angeles 'riots', for example (Griffin, 1992). It has become an element of common sense in the British media to refer to the supposedly novel and rising incidence of 'mindless violence' amongst young white (and African-Caribbean) working-class men. Panics over the use of ecstasy are more recent and currently confined to Britain. Deaths connected with ecstasy are far fewer than those associated with alcohol, but the drug has been demonized following the death of Leah Betts, the teenage daughter of a police inspector (Sharkey, 1996). Panics over 'Generation X' focus on a cultural form which has been associated with the young heterosexual, relatively affluent children of the white middle-classes on both sides of the Atlantic.

In all of these panics, specific groups of young people are singled out for attention, and the focus of concern often deals with some aspect of young people's relationship to the cycle of consumption, production and reproduction. 'Problem teens' appear as a source of (adult) concern over (specific) young people's disordered relationship with consumption (e.g. drug use and food), reproduction (e.g. 'teen mothers') and/or production, which usually refers to the transition from education to the job market (e.g. slackers, youth crime). There are many more examples one could give. The continued development of a feminist perspective on the specific relation of youth to the cycle of consumption, production and reproduction is important, partly because such representations of youth are so profoundly gendered and sexualized. However, it is not possible to concentrate solely on gender, age and sexuality without also considering relations of 'race', class and disability. 'Youth' itself is constructed in monolithic terms as a relatively uniform age stage, but notions of 'deviance', 'disorder' and 'problem youth' are almost always about making distinctions between specific groups of young people. The monolithic category of 'youth' can be mobilized to obscure differences between groups of young people and especially those based on social relations around gender, 'race', class, sexuality or disability.

Youth, Freedom and Control: G. Stanley Hall and 'Discovery' of Adolescence

When adolescence first emerged as an ideological construct in the late nineteenth century, many elements of contemporary representations around youth were forged. G. Stanley Hall's two-volume text 'On Adolescence' is generally taken as the key moment of 'discovery', but Hall was merely a focus for a diverse range of discourses around youth from education, medicine, criminology, the child study movement, other liberal reformers, and the emerging fields of psychology and psychoanalysis (Hall, 1904). Adolescence emerged as a period characterized by inevitable physiological changes and hormonal turmoil, instigated by the onset of puberty

(Griffin, 1993). What came to be known as the Storm and Stress model of adolescence had its origins here. As an age stage, adolescence is fundamentally sexualized, and assumed to be primarily determined by biological forces. Young people's relationship to reproduction (in the sense of reproducing offspring) is central to this construction. Adolescence is also distinctly gendered, since its starting point, the onset of puberty, is assumed to be quite different for young women and men, who are distinguished by their different roles in reproduction. Menarche, or the onset of menstruation, is a (relatively) discrete event associated with the ability to reproduce. The onset of puberty for males is far more fragmented and uncertain, and scarcely emerges as a distinct moment at all (Laslett, 1971). Discourses of freedom and control were central to Hall's construction of adolescence, and they remain with us as key elements in dominant regimes for the representation and management of youth. For Hall, freedom and control were especially associated with 'emerging' adolescent sexuality, a theme which is familiar from the Storm and Stress model. As I have argued elsewhere: 'Hall advocated a contradictory mixture of freedom and control: freedom would allow adolescents to discover their potentialities, and control would be necessary to establish order and self-discipline' (Griffin, 1993: 16). For Hall, sexual impulses provided a particular focus for the management of adolescent freedom and control, represented in a specifically gendered and heterosexualized form (Hall, 1904).

The period of adolescence is constituted as an inevitable, biologically-driven conflict between youthful instincts and desires (for sex, rebellion, freedom from adult control) and the need to control such desires. Adults, in the form of parents, teachers, youth workers and employers, should be the first to assert such necessary surveillance and control, but successful socialization into adulthood is characterized by the development of 'appropriate' techniques of *self-*surveillance and *self-*control. Such regimes are familiar from the texts of feminists who have drawn on Foucault's work on the care of the self (e.g. Probyn, 1993). A great deal of feminist work has also examined the damaging implications of regimes of sexualized self-surveillance for women (Bordo, 1993; Winship, 1981).

Battles over freedom and control are to be fought out in the realm of leisure, education, family life, sexuality and waged work, then, but *within* the (gendered, racialized, etc.) adolescent self. Adolescence is represented as a period in which the desire for 'freedom' (especially separation from the family of origin) is seen as inevitable, and 'defiance' is assumed to accompany such inevitable desires almost as a matter of course. Such 'defiance' is viewed through a lens of 'race' and class, however, as well as gender and sexuality. The management of youth/adolescence for young people and for adults is caught in a tension between discourses of freedom and control.

So whilst 'defiance' and 'rebellion' are seen as inevitable consequences of youth, only certain forms of 'defiance' (varying with gender, etc.) will be tolerated. Young people's 'freedoms' and 'rebellions', such as attempts at independence from the family of origin, for example, are bounded by the constraints associated with adult status and adult positions in the production/reproduction/consumption cycle. Such adult positions are fundamentally gendered.

When 'trouble' does occur, in certain historical and political contexts this supposedly inevitable youthful defiance is represented as intolerable and becomes a focus for adult intervention. It is this area of (adult) concern into which the US Specialty Schools and wilderness programmes mentioned at the start of this article aim to intervene. Adverts for such establishments proclaim their intention to help 'bright but unmotivated' and 'out of control teens', and to bring them 'out of their fantasy world and back to reality' (Griffin, 1996). Regimes of (external, adult) control, sometimes called 'therapy' or 'education', move into place. The desired outcome here is the 'learning' of (self-)control by the 'problem teen' in order to bring them back onto the 'right' path towards academic achievement, professional success, family unity, alcohol and drug detoxification, stable heterosexual relationships (especially for young women) and other forms of 'appropriate' behaviour. Key indices of successful treatment might include the cessation of various forms of 'disordered consumption' on the part of the young person, whether of alcohol, drugs or (for young women) sex and/or food. Distinct futures are mapped out as 'appropriate' for different groups of young people, such that what might be seen as quite acceptable for a white middle-class male (university education, professional career, head of nuclear family household in affluent suburb) would definitely not be seen as relevant for his Black, working-class and/or female peers.

'Trouble' from teenagers (for adults) is represented as inevitable ('part of growing up') but only to be tolerated within certain limits bounded in part by discourses of freedom and control. The latter construct a series of impossible contradictions between the inevitable adolescent separation from the family of origin and the need to maintain family unity (and dependence). Such contradictions are played out at the psychological, social, cultural and economic levels. It is this sense of adolescence as a battleground between 'freedom' and 'control' characterized by disordered paths of transition and disordered patterns of consumption that I want to turn to now by considering the particular position(s) of young women within this arena.

Young Women and Consumption: Stories of Desire, Freedom, Surveillance and Control

Debates about consumerism and women's relationship to the circuit of production, reproduction and consumption have undergone a series of shifts since the 1950s. Mainstream British youth research warned against the dangers of 'mass culture' (a US import) luring young people away from traditional British values with a culture of glamour, excitement and novelty (e.g. Veness, 1962; Carter, 1962). For young women, the dangers and thrills associated with such 'mass culture' were located in the realm of the sexual and the domestic, disrupting 'normal' transitions to heterosexual courtship, marriage and motherhood. These assumptions permeated even the apparently more radical field of cultural studies (Hoggart, 1957). Young people, working-class youth and young women were assumed to be most 'at risk' here, more readily duped by those marketing to the new 'teenage consumer' (Abrams, 1959).

The late 1960s onwards have seen a series of increasingly sophisticated subversions of dominant cultural forms and products by various groups of young people in the realms of music, fashion and art, often blurring and transforming the boundaries between passive consumer and active producer of artifacts (Willis *et al.*, 1990). Appropriations and re-appropriations of earlier styles, nostalgia used in a conscious and humorous way, close associations between musical styles, cultural forms and political activities have all appeared (and re-appeared) over the past thirty years or so. Youthful consumption has been represented as passive conformism, creative resistance, selfish desire, an active construction of the self via the body, in complex ways that have moved a long way from the supposedly gullible teenage consumer of the 1950s (Nava, 1992).

As a practice, consumerism is fundamentally gendered, sexualized, class and race-specific. Mica Nava, in her useful review of recent theorizations of consumerism, argues that such theorizations need to be understood in political and intellectual context (Nava, 1992). During the 1950s and 1960s, conservative, Marxist and early feminist critics (e.g. Friedan, 1965) condemned mass consumption in elitist terms, predicating their arguments on the notion of the passive consumer. During the late 1960s and into the 1970s and 1980s, consumption came to be celebrated by radicals as a form of creative appropriation of, even resistance to, dominant 'high' culture. In youth research, the work of Marxists and feminists concerned with youth cultures and subcultures were highly influential (Hall and Jefferson, 1975). The active 'creative' consumers that provided the focus for much of this research tended to be white, male and heterosexual, either middle-class hippies or working-class 'lads' (e.g. Willis, 1978).

Angela McRobbie's work adopted the perspective of young (white, working-class, heterosexual) women in her studies of *Jackie*, the magazine for teenage girls, and of working-class cultures of femininity, which revolved around the girls' bedrooms rather than the street (McRobbie, 1978; McRobbie and Garber 1975). More recent work has exploded that distinction between passive consumer and creative cultural warrior, examining intersections of 'race', class, gender and sexuality in a range of youthful consumption patterns and cultural practices (Jones, 1988; McRobbie, 1989).

Much of this work has focused on the position of young people in general, and young women in particular, as consuming subjects of material goods. Similarly, feminist analyses of women's relation to the production/repro-duction/consumption cycle have concentrated on women's positions as consuming, producing and/or reproducing subjects. What I have argued here and elsewhere is that *young* women (and young men) occupy distinct positions as consumers in relation to discourses of freedom and control in the context of the dominant Storm and Stress model of adolescence (cf. Griffin, 1993). For young people, the cycle of production/reproduction/consumption is represented as something to be entered via a series of tran-sitions into a set of subject positions associated with adult status. For young men, the most crucial subject position often revolves around a job, and for young women, their relation to men and family life as wives and mothers will appear as most important (Jones and Wallace, 1992). Recent reductions in youth employment rates, the benefits system and state pro-vision in the fields of housing, health, leisure, education and training have disrupted these moments of transition to a significant extent, and it is no longer clear how useful such conceptualizations are (or were) in relation to young people's experience of 'growing up'.

Disrupted Transitions: Growing Up in the 1990s

Radical and mainstream youth researchers during the 1980s were arguing that young people in many 'advanced' industrialized nations were facing a crisis due to rising levels of youth unemployment, welfare and education cuts, and a variety of cultural and political changes (Griffin, 1993). Paul Willis, for example, argued in 1984 that rising youth unemployment in Britain would (and had already begun to) seriously disrupt crucial transi-tions from school into the job market and into heterosexual courtship, marriage and parenthood for working-class youth (Willis, 1984). In addition, the growing independence of young women as a consequence of the 'mainstreaming' of feminism has been seen as a contributory element in this respect. Evidence is mixed however, and although increasing numbers of young single working-class women are becoming pregnant, the proportion of the population marrying has not dropped significantly, although on average people are marrying later and divorcing sooner than they did twenty years ago (Abercrombie *et al.*, 1994). Some groups of young people may appear to be withdrawing from traditional paths into the labour market and married life, although this is scarcely a matter of 'free choice'. Bob Hollands' study of leisure activities in the north-east of England, for example, indicates that in an area of high unemployment, many young heterosexual working-class whites delay the entry to the adult world of marriage and full-time waged work. They scrape together money, continue to live with their parents, and 'go out' at weekends, often in single sex groups, to pubs and clubs in the city centre (Hollands, 1995). Rising unemployment, welfare and education cuts, and over a decade of right-wing government on both sides of the Atlantic have undoubtedly had a disruptive impact on the (never entirely smooth) transition to adulthood. The 1980s and 1990s have been a period of relative crisis for those managing 'troubled teens' through this period of constructed transition.

In Britain, the seeds of such disrupted transitions and a growing sense of adult concern were evident prior to the 1980s: indeed the history of 'adolescence' has been a story of periodic moral panics (Pearson, 1983). Official concern over the possible effects of youth unemployment on the young people concerned and on 'society as a whole' was reflected in the rhetoric behind the various youth training and job creation schemes developed by Jim Callaghan's Labour government during the mid-1970s. Thatcherism brought a sharp rise in youth unemployment levels, especially amongst Black and white working-class youth, and a new set of schemes which included an increasing element of coercion. From the mid-1980s, such concerns coalesced in the context of more widespread anxieties about 'the state of the nation's youth' which was reflected (in different ways) in texts by radical and mainstream youth researchers (Griffin, 1993). Concern focused at first on working-class young people and the possibility of mass withdrawal from the (dwindling) job market, especially amongst young men. Apparent increases in rates of 'teenage pregnancy' provided the focus for concern over the lives of young working-class women (Phoenix, 1990).

Panics over the detrimental impact of Thatcherite policies on young people revolved around their potentially disrupted entry into 'adult' positions within the production/reproduction/consumption cycle. In 1986 for example, sociologists Frank Coffield, Carol Borrill and Sarah Marshall argued that what they termed the 'unofficial, unwritten [social] contract' between young people and society had broken down in most western countries. This state of affairs had been brought about by 'alarming increases' in youth unemployment in the late 1970s and early 1980s

(Coffield *et al.*, 1986: 203). By 'social contract', Coffield and his colleagues meant more than young people's position in the labour market. They also used this term to refer to 'the means whereby society seeks to integrate each new generation of young people into all its essential activities, which include the formation of new families and the raising of children' (1986: 203–4). In this liberal account of young people's entry into the circuit of production, reproduction and consumption, power, poverty and exploitation figure as integral to the analysis. Gender is not ignored as an organizing force in social relations, and positive discrimination for young women and increased participation by young people in policy making are suggested as possible means of forging a new and alternative 'social contract' (Coffield *et al.*, 1986). The aim of this approach is to smooth over and improve disrupted transitions to adulthood for all young people. 'Shit jobs and govvy schemes' might improve, and youth unemployment would decrease dramatically in Coffield's ideal world, but marriage and the institution of heterosexuality would probably remain all but unchanged. Mainstream analyses of this kind, whilst they do recognize the different relationships of young people to the production/reproduction/consumption cycle, still operate with relatively traditional notions of consumption.

As Gill Jones and Clare Wallace have pointed out in their analysis of 'Youth, Family Life and Citizenship', young people are drawn into the consumer market at an increasingly early age (Jones and Wallace, 1992). It is not that children and young people have *no* involvement with the circuit of production/reproduction/consumption. Far from it, they are increasingly likely to be targeted as consumers, as exemplified by recent attempts in Britain to sell new computer technologies (hard- and software) by presenting them as Xmas presents with an 'educational' function for children (usually boys). What is important about youth as an age stage is that it is represented as the moment at which we enter (or are supposed to enter) the cycle of production/reproduction/consumption *as adults*. Jones and Wallace recognize this when they include poverty and homelessness in their analysis of young people's positions as 'consumer citizens'. Such an inclusion is relatively unusual, since considerations of youthful consumption have tended to be shaped by Cohen's work on 'teenage consumers', and by studies on youth cultures and subcultures and from the sociology of leisure. The main focus of such analyses has been the consumption of material goods and services (e.g. clothes, films, music) and the cultural meanings associated with various patterns of consumption (e.g. Hebdige, 1979). If we extend the concept of youthful (and adult) consumption to include poverty and homelessness, it is possible to locate consumption as part of a cycle which incorporates transitions into the (hetero)sexual and marriages marketplace(s) as well as the job market.

The literature on young people and consumption tends to be characterized by debates over whether (different groups of) young people can be viewed as active consumers or relatively passive victims of pressures to consume (Nava, 1992; cf. Miles, 1995). Such debates often founder on questions of representation: who decides that specific consumption patterns and cultural forms are creative, while others collude with market forces? The 1970s and 1980s brought a new perspective to bear on analyses of culture and consumption: ideas derived from post-structuralism and postmodernism. Complexity, fragmentation, multiplicity and transformation were emphasized, and styles, consumption patterns and cultural practices were less securely tied to specific gender, class and ethnic youth groups (Hebdige, 1979).

By the 1990s, it has become less common (and increasingly difficult) to make clear-cut associations between specific groups of young people and particular styles and patterns of material consumption. Rising youth unemployment and increasingly complex global cultures and technological forms have undermined some of the key certainties on which analyses of youth cultural styles were founded. However, young women have always been relatively marginal to these analyses, as have Black youth, young people with disabilities, gay, lesbian and bisexual young people. Just as young women's voices began to be heard in youth research during the 1980s, arguments derived from postmodernism emerged to question some of the founding assumptions about relationships between culture, identity, structure and agency (Griffin, 1993). Feminists working in this area have had to do some hard thinking. How do feminists working as researchers appreciate the complexities and priorities of young people's lives amongst those who have been relatively silenced and marginalized, both with youth research and in society more generally? In a climate where many issues around academic researchers 'speaking for' others are problematized, there are no easy solutions.

Many mainstream youth researchers have shifted their focus as a consequence of rising youth unemployment and other major social and economic changes. Jones and Wallace, for example, use the notion of citizenship to refer to inclusion or exclusion in mainstream adult society, with its associated rights and responsibilities (Jones and Wallace, 1992). The concept of citizenship removes the biological discourse associated with 'adolescence' and therefore with adult status, and it allows us to represent certain young people as positioned on the margins of citizenship, or excluded altogether. Young people with disabilities or mental health problems, young homeless people and the young unemployed are examples of such marginalized groups. Jones and Wallace cite the work of Ruth Lister (1990), who includes young women and others who have not achieved financial independence in this group that are excluded from full citizenship. For feminists, citizenship can provide a useful means of thinking about differential access to social, economic and political participation, and it may be especially relevant to discourses of youthful 'disaffection' and 'disenfranchisement' (Bhavnani, 1991). The concept of citizenship enables us to think about diverse elements of the consumption/production/reproduction cycle simultaneously.

The notion of citizenship avoids the tendency to construct young people as either active or passive consumers, but it rests on a dominant concept of the 'citizen', which in itself is a product of a precise historical and political moment. Jones and Wallace do not deconstruct the notion of the citizen to any significant extent. The construct of citizenship is also less valuable as a means of understanding social relations around sexuality, which are central to the management of the transition to adulthood and entry to the production/reproduction/consumption cycle for young people – and especially for young women.

Young women who are identified as having 'disordered' patterns of consumption, whether of food, sex, illegal drugs or alcohol, can appear as a particular problem because their path through traditional routes to marriage, motherhood and a job are blocked. Such discourses construct them in an active mode – as 'food refusers' or 'ever-pregnant teens', but also passively – for mixing with a 'bad crowd', or being 'at risk' of getting pregnant (Griffin, 1993). These discourses also represent young women with 'problems' (and *as* problems) through 'disorders' of consumption and reproduction, and this is especially relevant to panics over young single women with children (Phoenix, 1990).

My argument then, is that we need, as feminists, to move from debates over whether young women are oppressed as passive consumers, or whether they have a potential to create new lives and new selves by transforming, appropriating and reappropriating pervasive patterns and modes of consumption. Our concept of consumption needs to include more than material goods and services and the various symbolic meanings associated with particular consumption patterns. The relation of consumption to the (gendered, sexualized and racialized) body and to the self are equally important. Young people's use of substances such as illegal drugs, alcohol, tobacco and food extend the notion of consumption into the domains of health, medicine and therapy. It is important to consider how various groups of young women (and men) are represented in specific contexts as consumers, and especially as disordered consumers, and the ways in which such representations and the associated regimes of management and treatment are gendered, sexualized, racialized and class-specific.

In a recent study of young people's approaches to health, Julia Brannen, Kathryn Dodd, Ann Oakley and Pamela Storey interviewed young people aged 16 and their parents about health-related behaviours, attitudes and negotiations of areas of potential conflict (Brannen *et al.*, 1994). The resulting text operates from the set of discourses described above, although this is scarcely surprising, since the study was funded by the Department of Health based on a research design which reflected 'common sense' assumptions about young people, health, family life and transitions to adulthood. Brannen and her colleagues follow many other academic and policy texts in this field by associating potential 'teenage problems' and 'risky behaviours' (to health in this case) with a set of practices involving consumption: drinking alcohol, smoking cigarettes and taking illegal drugs. They also refer to certain forms of sexual behaviour (especially 'unprotected' heterosexual intercourse outside marriage and/or under the legal age of consent) in terms of potential risk – particularly for young women. Sex is part of the transition into adult positions in the production/reproduction/consumption cycle, since in this form it relates both to consumption and reproduction. Young (and not so young) women are items of consumption for young (and not so young) men (Griffin *et al.*, 1982), and part of the 'risk' posed by unprotected heterosexual intercourse for young women is that of pregnancy. In the Brannen *et al.* study, interviews with young people and their parents illustrate the extent to which these 'risky' activities are often the focus of considerable negotiation and conflict in households. It is from this arena of dispute over consumption and the transition to adult status that the US Specialty Schools mentioned at the start of this article emerged as a broader social response to the problem of 'troubled teens'.

Specialty Schools and associated programmes for 'troubled teens' are a distinctly North American (specifically US) phenomenon. They are predominantly residential, fee-paying and frequently recruit their clientele via approaches to affluent parents through advertising. They do not all work closely with the established, accredited and professionally regulated state health care or educational system, although scholarships and state or federal grants are available. There is, of course, a long tradition of sending the children and young people of affluent parents away to school in other industrialized nations: the English public school system is an obvious point of comparison here. Nor is it unusual to view the rural environment as an area imbued with curative properties or potential for the rehabilitation of troubled youthful psyches (Kett, 1977; Gillis, 1974). In contemporary youth work, outdoor activities form a vital element in both more traditional 'character-building' programmes and progressive group-focused schemes (Ford, 1993).

The notion of therapeutic help for young people with 'emotional and behaviour difficulties' is commonplace on both sides of the Atlantic, as are 'remedial' regimes for 'underachieving' youth in the educational domain. In Britain, these systems might focus on working-class and/or Black youth, however, as would correctional institutions for those who truant from school or 'get in trouble' with the police (Griffin, 1993). What is unusual about these US Specialty Schools is the combination of so many key elements of discourses around 'troubled youth' and associated regimes of treatment, rehabilitation, care *and* control (Griffin, 1996).

Summary

How are we to understand these contemporary constructions of young people, and especially young women, in texts from all parts of the political spectrum? Left and Right appear to argue that rising youth unemployment, welfare cuts and myriad cultural and technical changes have disrupted traditional transitions to adulthood, although such developments are greeted in very different ways. If entry to 'adult' positions in the cycle of consumption, production, reproduction and distribution are being disrupted for increasing numbers of young people in the 'First World', especially if they are working-class and/or Black, what are the implications for feminist theories and practices? It is no longer possible to develop simplistic constructions of (certain groups of) young women solely as passive victims of oppression, pushed into heterosexual marriage and/or motherhood, and gullible recipients of a range of products aimed at a young female market. Nor is it possible to portray all young women as in creative resistance against the forces of patriarchal capitalism, or as active consumers asserting their desires and freedoms in an open marketplace.

For many young women (and young men), dominant representations of 'normal' family life appear as pervasive if increasingly distant images, strongly associated with a particular set of consumer goods – including a VCR and a CD player (cf. Wallace, 1987). Their paths to that Shangri-la may be blocked, and the rosy-tinted image may not be accepted so uncritically by many young people. Here, perhaps, we have one source of the recent moral panics over disrupted transitions to adulthood. What if the bait (steady job, nice things, lovely home/car/baby/husband) fails to materialize at all? For many feminists, the 'bait' of heterosexuality, marriage, motherhood and a shit job has never signified much more than a series of traps, but faced with apparently significant disruptions to the circuit of consumption, production, reproduction and distribution, other uncertainties emerge.

Notes

Christine Griffin teaches social psychology at the University of Birmingham. Her research interests include the 'transition to adulthood', especially for young women, and feminist approaches to qualitative research. She is author of *Typical Girls? Young Women from School to the Job Market* (1985, London: Routledge & Kegan Paul), and *Representations of Youth: The Study of Youth and Adolescence in Britain and America* (1993, Cambridge: Polity Press). She is one of the founding editors of the journal *Feminism and Psychology*, and is currently working on an ESRC-funded study of the relationships between unemployment, crime and masculinity amongst long-term unemployed male offenders with Sara Willott.

References

ABERCROMBIE, N., WARDLE, A., SOOTHILL, K., URRY, J. and WALBY, S. (1994) *Contemporary British Society* Cambridge: Polity Press. Second edition.

ABRAMS, M. (1959) *The Teenage Consumer* London: Routledge & Kegan Paul.

BHAVNANI, K.-K. (1991) *Talking Politics: A Psychological Framing for Views from Youth in Britain* Cambridge: Cambridge University Press.

BORDO, S. (1993) *Unbearable Weight: Feminism, Western Culture and the Body* Berkeley: University of California Press.

BRANNEN, J., DODD, K., OAKLEY, A. and STOREY, P. (1994) *Young People, Health and Family Life* Buckingham: Open University Press.

CAIN, M. (ed.) (1989) *Growing Up Good: Policing the Behaviour of Girls in Europe* London: Sage.

CARTER, M. (1962) *Home, School and Work* London: Pergamon Press.

COFFIELD, F., BORRILL, C. and MARSHALL, S. (1986) *Growing Up at the Margins* Milton Keynes: Open University Press.

CONGER, J. (1979) *Adolescence: A Generation Under Pressure* London: Harper & Row.

CONNELL, R.W. (1993) *Masculinities* Cambridge: Polity Press.

FORD, L. (1993) 'The Sierra Nevada expedition', *Youth and Policy*, Vol. 40, No. 2, pp. 76–80.

FRIEDAN, B. (1965) *The Feminine Mystique* Harmondsworth: Penguin.

GILLIS, J. (1974) *Youth and History: Tradition and Change in European Age Relations: 1770–Present* New York: Academic Press.

GRIFFIN, C. (1982) 'The good, the bad and the ugly: images of young women in the labour market.' CCCS, Birmingham University, Occasional paper.

GRIFFIN, C. (1988) 'Youth research: young women and the "gang of lads" model' in Hazekamp, Meeus and te Poel editors *European Contributions to Youth Research* Amsterdam: Free University Press.

GRIFFIN, C. (1992) 'Fear of a Black (and working class) planet: young women and the racialisation of reproductive politics' *Feminism and Psychology*, Vol. 2, No. 3, pp. 491–4.

GRIFFIN, C. (1993) *Representations of Youth: The Study of Youth and Adolescence in Britain and America* Cambridge: Polity Press.

GRIFFIN, C. (1996) 'The management of disorders of transition and consumption in young people: when gender is (apparently) absent', Women and Psychology conference, University of West of England, 2–4 July.

GRIFFIN, C., HOBSON, D., MACINTOSH, S. and McCABE, T. (1982) 'Women and leisure' in **Hargreaves** editor *Sport, Culture and Ideology* London: Routledge & Kegan Paul.

GRIFFIN, C. and PHOENIX, A. (1994) 'The relationship between qualitative and quantitative research' *Journal of Community and Applied Social Psychology* Vol. 4, pp. 287–98.

HALL, G. Stanley (1904) *Adolescence: Its Psychology and Its Relation to Physiology, Anthropology, Sociology, Sex, Crime, Religion and Education* New York: D. Appleton & Co.

HALL, S. and JEFFERSON, T. (eds) (1975) *Resistance Through Rituals: Youth Subcultures in Post-war Britain* London: Hutchinson.

HEBDIGE, D. (1979) *Subcultures: The Meaning of Style* London: Methuen.

HOGGART, R. (1957) *The Uses of Literacy* Harmondsworth: Penguin.

HOLLANDS, R. G. (1995) *Friday Night, Saturday Night: Youth Cultural Identification in the Post-industrial City* Newcastle-upon-Tyne: Department of Social Policy, University of Newcastle.

JEFFS, T. and SMITH, M. (1994) 'Young people, youth work and a new authoritarianism' *Youth and Policy* Vol. 46, No. 3, pp. 17–32.

JONES, G. and WALLACE, C. (1992) *Youth, Family and Citizenship* Buckingham: Open University Press.

JONES, S. (1988) *Black Culture, White Youth: The Reggae Tradition from JA to UK* London: Macmillan.

KETT, J. (1977) *Rites of Passage: Adolescence in America: 1790 to the Present* New York: Basic Books.

LASLETT, P. (1971) 'Age of menarche in Europe since the 18th century' *Journal of Interdisciplinary History* Vol. 2, No. 2, pp. 221–36.

LEES, S. (1986) *Losing Out: Sexuality and Adolescent Girls* London: Hutchinson.

LISTER, R. (1990) 'Women, economic dependency and citizenship' *Journal of Social Policy* Vol. 19, No. 4, 445–67.

McROBBIE, A. (1978) 'Working class girls and the culture of femininity' in Women's Studies Group, CCCS, editors *Women Take Issue: Aspects of Women's Subordination* London: Hutchinson.

McROBBIE, A. (ed.) (1989) *Zoot Suits and Second-hand Dresses: An Anthology of Fashion and Music* London: Macmillan.

McROBBIE, A. and GARBER, J. (1975) 'Girls and subcultures: an exploration' in **Hall** and **Jefferson**, editors *Resistance Through Rituals*.

MILES, S. (1995) 'Towards an understanding of the relationship between youth identities and consumer culture' *Youth and Policy* Vol. 51, No. 4, pp. 35–45.

MOHANTY, C.T., RUSSO, A. and TORRES, L. (eds) (1991) *Third World Women and the Politics of Feminism* Indianapolis: Indiana University Press.

MUNCIE, J. (1984) *The Trouble with Kids Today: Youth and Crime in Post-war Britain* London: Hutchinson.

NAVA, M. (1992) *Changing Cultures: Feminism, Youth and Consumerism* London: Macmillan.

PEARSON, G. (1983) *Hooligan: A History of Respectable Fears* London: Macmillan.

PHOENIX, A. (1990) *Young Mothers?* Cambridge: Polity Press.

PROBYN, E. (1993) *Sexing the Self: Gendered Positions in Cultural Studies* London: Routledge.

RICHARDSON, D. and ROBINSON, V. (eds) (1992) *Introducing Women's Studies* London: Macmillan.

SHARKEY, A. (1996) 'Sorted or distorted?' *Guardian*, 26 January.

TONG, R. (1989) *Feminist Thought: A Comprehensive Introduction* London: Routledge.

VENESS, T. (1962) *School Leavers* London: Methuen.

WALLACE, C. (1987) *For Richer, For Poorer: Growing Up in and out of Work* London: Tavistock.

WILLIS, P. (1978) *Profane Culture* London: Routledge & Kegan Paul.

WILLIS, P. (1984) 'Youth unemployment: thinking the unthinkable' *Youth and Policy* Vol. 2, No. 4, pp. 17–36.

WILLIS, P., JONES, S., CANAAN, J. and HURD, G. (1990) *Common Culture: Symbolic Work at Play in the Everyday Cultures of the Young* Milton Keynes: Open University Press.

WINSHIP, J. (1981) 'Woman becomes an "individual": femininity and consumption in women's magazines 1954–1969' CCCS, Birmingham University, Occasional paper.

FEMINIST REVIEW NO 55, SPRING 1997, pp. 22–72

The Virtual Speculum in the New World Order[1]

Donna J. Haraway

Abstract

Beginning by reading a 1992 feminist appropriation of Michelangelo's *Creation of Adam* – in a cartoon in which the finger of a nude Adamic woman touches a computer keyboard, while the god-like VDT screen shows a disembodied fetus – 'Virtual Speculum' argues for a broader conception of 'new reproductive technologies' in order to foreground justice and freedom projects for differently situated women in the New World Order. Broadly conceptualized reproductive practices must be central to social theory in general, and to technoscience studies in particular. Tying together the politics of self help and women's health movements in the United States in the 1970s with positions on reproductive freedom articulated within the Legal Defense and Educational Fund of the NAACP in the 1990s, the paper examines recent work in feminist science studies in several disciplinary and activist locations. Statistical analysis and ethnography emerge as critical feminist technologies for producing convincing representations of the reproduction of inequality. Untangling the semiotic and political–economic dialectics of invisibility and hypervisibility, 'Virtual Speculum' concludes by linking the well-surveyed amniotic fluid of on-screen fetuses and the off-frame diarrhea of uncounted and underfed infants in regimes of flexible accumulation and structural adjustment.

Keywords

feminism; reproduction; freedom projects; visual culture; ethnography; science studies; reproductive technologies; United States; Brazil

These are the days of miracle and wonder
This is the long distance call
The way the camera follows us in slo-mo
The way we look to us all
The way we look to a distant constellation
That's dying in a corner of the sky
These are the days of miracle and wonder
And don't cry, baby, don't cry

It was a dry wind
And it swept across the desert

And it curled into the circle of birth
And the dead sand
Falling on the children
The mothers and the fathers
And the automatic earth
. . .
Medicine is magical and magical is art
The Boy in the Bubble
And the baby with the baboon heart

And I believe
These are the days of lasers in the jungle
Lasers in the jungle somewhere
Staccato signals of constant information
A loose affiliation of millionaires
And billionaires and baby
These are the days of miracle and wonder
This is the long-distance call
© 1986 Paul Simon/Paul Simon Music (BMI)

In its ability to embody the union of science and nature,
the embryo might be described as a cyborg kinship entity.

Sarah Franklin (1993a: 131)

The fetus and the planet earth are sibling seed worlds in technoscience. If NASA photographs of the blue, cloud-swathed whole earth are icons for the emergence of global, national and local struggles over a recent natural–technical object of knowledge called the environment, then the ubiquitous images of glowing, free-floating, human fetuses condense and intensify struggles over an equally new and disruptive technoscientific object of knowledge, namely 'life itself' (Franklin, 1993b; Duden, 1993; Foucault, 1978). Life as a system to be managed – a field of operations constituted by scientists, artists, cartoonists, community activists, mothers, anthropologists, fathers, publishers, engineers, legislators, ethicists, industrialists, bankers, doctors, genetic counsellors, judges, insurers, priests, and all their relatives – has a very recent pedigree. The fetus and the whole earth concentrate the elixir of life as a complex system; that is, of life itself. Each image is about the origin of life in a postmodern world.

Both the whole earth and the fetus owe their existence as public objects to visualizing technologies. These technologies include computers, video cameras, satellites, sonography machines, optical fibre technology, television, micro cinematography and much more. The global fetus and the spherical whole earth both exist because of, and inside of, technoscientific visual culture. Yet, I think, both signify touch. Both provoke yearning for the physical sensuousness of a wet and blue-green earth and a soft, fleshy child. That is why these images are so ideologically powerful. They signify the immediately natural and embodied, over and against the constructed and disembodied. These latter qualities are charged against the supposedly violating, distancing, scopic eye of science and theory. The audiences who find the glowing fetal and terran spheres to be powerful signifiers of touch are themselves partially constituted as subjects in the material–semiotic process of viewing. The system of ideological oppositions between signifiers of touch and vision remains stubbornly essential to political and scientific debate in modern western culture. This system is a field of meanings that elaborates the ideological tension between body and machine, nature and culture, female and male, tropical and northern, coloured and white, traditional and modern, and lived experience and dominating objectification.

The Sacred and the Comic

Sometimes complicitous, sometimes exuberantly creative, western feminists have had little choice about operating in the charged field of oppositional meanings structured around vision and touch. Small wonder, then, that feminists in science studies are natural deconstructionists, who resolutely chart fields of meanings that unsettle these oppositions, these set ups that frame human and non-human technoscientific actors and sentence them to terminal ideological confinement (Treichler and Cartwright, 1992). Because the fruit issuing from such confinement is toxic, let us try to reconceive some of the key origin stories about human life that congeal around the images of the fetus. In many domains in contemporary European and US cultures, the fetus functions as a kind of metonym, seed crystal, or icon for configurations of person, family, nation, origin, choice, life and future. As the German historian of the body Barbara Duden put it, the fetus functions as a modern 'sacrum', i.e., as an object in which the transcendent appears. The fetus as sacrum is the repository of heterogeneous people's stories, hopes and imprecations. Attentive to the wavering opposition between the sacred versus the comic, the sacramental versus the vulgar, scientific illustration versus advertising, art versus pornography, the body of scientific truth versus the caricature of the popular joke, the power of medicine versus the insult of death, I want to proceed here by relocating the fetal sacrum onto its comic twin.

In this task, I am instructed by feminists who have studied in the school of the masters. Two feminist cartoons separated by twenty years, and a missing image that cannot be a joke, will concern me most in this essay's effort to read the comics in technoscience. Set in the context of struggles over the terms, agents and contents of human reproduction, all three of my

Figure 1 Anne Kelly. *The Virtual Speculum*. Kelly's cartoon illustrated an article in a special issue on reproductive technology of a Norwegian feminist journal (Stabel, 1992: 44).

images trouble a reductionist sense of 'reproductive technologies'. Instead, the images are about a specifically feminist concept called 'reproductive freedom'. From the point of view of feminist science studies, freedom projects are what make technical projects make sense – with all the specificity, ambiguity, complexity and contradiction inherent in technoscience. Science projects are civics projects; they remake citizens. Technoscientific liberty is the goal (Flower, n.d.). Keep your eyes on the prize (Hampton 1986–87).

The first image, a cartoon by Anne Kelly that I have named the *Virtual Speculum*, is a representation of Michelangelo's painting of the *Creation of Adam* on the ceiling of the Sistine Chapel. The *Virtual Speculum* is a caricature in the potent political tradition of 'literal' reversals, which excavate the latent and implicit oppositions that made the original picture work. In Kelly's version, a female nude is in the position of Adam, whose hand is extended to the creative interface with, not God the Father, but a keyboard for a computer whose display screen shows the global digital fetus in its amniotic sac. A female Adam, the young nude woman is in the position of the first man. Kelly's figure is not Eve, who was made from Adam and in relation to his need.[2] In the *Virtual Speculum*, the woman is in direct relation to the source of life itself.

The cartoon seems to resonate in an echo chamber with a Bell Telephone advertisement on US television in the early 1990s, which urged potential long-distance customers 'to reach out and touch someone'. The racial-ethnic markings of the cast of characters varied in different versions of the ad. The visual text shows a pregnant woman, who is undergoing

**Figure 2 Michelangelo. *The Creation of Adam,*
Sistine Chapel, 1511-12**

ultrasonographic visualization of her fetus, telephoning her husband, the father of the fetus, to describe for him the first spectral appearance of his issue. The description is performative; i.e., the object described comes into existence, experientially, for all the participants in the drama. Fathers, mothers and children are constituted as subjects and objects for each other and the television audience. Life itself becomes an object of experience, which can be shared and memorialized. Proving herself to be a literate citizen of technoscience, the pregnant woman interprets the moving gray, white and black blobs of the televised sonogram as a visually obvious, differentiated fetus. Family bonding is in full flower in Bell Telephone's garden of creation. Surrogate for the absent father, the mother touches the on-screen fetus, establishing a tactile link between both parents-to-be and child-to-be. Here are interactive television and video of a marvellous kind. The mother-to-be's voice on the phone and finger on the screen are literally the conduits for the eye of the father. These are the touch and the word that mediate life itself, that turn bodies and machines into eloquent witnesses and storytellers.

Through advertising, Bell Telephone puts us inside the dramatic scenarios of technology and entertainment, twins to biomedicine and art. In the ad, reproductive technology and the visual arts – historically bound to the specific kinds of observation practised in the gynaecological exam and the life-drawing class – come together through the circles of mimesis built into communications practices in the New World Order. Life copies art copies technology copies communication copies life itself. Television, sonography, computer video display and the telephone are all apparatuses for the production of the nuclear family on screen. Voice and touch are brought into life on screen.

Kelly's cartoon works off of the fact, which remains odd to women of my menopausal generation, that in many contemporary technologically mediated pregnancies, expectant mothers emotionally bond with their fetuses through learning to see the developing child on screen during a sonogram (Rapp, forthcoming). And so do fathers, as well as members of Parliament and Congress (Hartouni, 1991; Franklin, 1993a). The sonogram is only one in a battery of visual artifacts that establish the fact of fetal life within political, personal and biomedical discourse. But obstetrical ultrasonography figures in powerful political–technical pedagogies for learning to see who exists in the world (Petchesky 1987). Selves and subjects are produced in such 'lived experiences'. Quickening, or the mother's testimony to the movement of the unseen child-to-be in her womb, has here neither the experiential nor epistemological authority it did, and does, under different historical modes of embodiment. In Kelly's version, the bonding produced by computer-mediated visualization also produces subjects and selves; the touch at the keyboard is generative – emotionally, materially and epistemologically. But things work both similarly and differently from the way they do on the Sistine Chapel ceiling or in the Bell Telephone TV advertisement.

In the *Virtual Speculum* the grayish blobs of the television sonogram have given place to the defined anatomical form of the free-floating fetus. Kelly's on-screen fetus is more like an *in vivo* movie, photograph or computer-graphic reconstruction – all of which are received at least partly within the conventions of post-Renaissance visual realism, which the blob-like sonographic image has great difficulty invoking. The televised sonogram is more like a biological monster movie, which one still has to learn to view even in the late twentieth century. By contrast, to those who learned how to see after the revolution in painting initiated in the fifteenth and sixteenth centuries in Northern and Southern Europe, the free-floating, anatomically sharp, perspectively registered fetal image appears self-evident at first viewing. Post-Renaissance anatomical realism and late twentieth-century computer-generated corporeal realism still share many, although not all, viewing conventions and epistemological assumptions.

The fetus like the one in *Virtual Speculum* is the iconic form that has been made so familiar by the exquisite, internationally distributed images produced by the Swedish biomedical photographer, Lennart Nilsson. Endoscopic intrauterine fetal visualization began in the 1950s, well before sonograms were part of the cultural terrain. The visible fetus became a public object with the April 1965 *Life* magazine cover featuring Nilsson's photograph of an intrauterine eighteen-week-old developing human being, encased in its bubble-like amniotic sac. The rest of the Nilsson photos in the 1965 *Life* story, 'The Drama of Life before Birth', were of extrauterine abortuses, beautifully lit and photographed in colour to become the visual embodiment of life at its origin. Not seen as abortuses, these gorgeous fetuses and their descendants signified life itself, in its transcendent essence and immanent embodiment. The visual image of the fetus is like the DNA double helix – not just a signifier of life, but also offered as the thing-in-itself. The visual fetus, like the gene, is a technoscientific sacrament. The sign becomes the thing itself in ordinary magico-secular transubstantiation.

Nilsson's images have spiked the visual landscape for the last thirty years, each time with announcements of originary art and technology, originary personal and scientific experience, and unique revelations bringing what was hidden into the light. Nilsson's photographs are simultaneously high art, scientific illustration, research tool and mass popular culture. The 1965 'Drama of Life before Birth' was followed by the popular coffee-table format book, *A Child Is Born* (Nilsson, 1977); the NOVA television special in 1983, 'The Miracle of Life'; the lavishly illustrated book (Nilsson, 1987) on the immune system, including images of developing fetuses, *The Body Victorious*; and the August 1990 *Life* cover photo of a seven-week-old fetus, with the caption, 'The First Pictures Ever of How Life Begins', and the accompanying story, 'The First Days of Creation' (Stabile, 1992). Finally, moving from conception through breast feeding, *A Child Is Born* was issued as a compact-disk adaptation, whose content-rich multimedia design offers interactive features as part of the visual fetal feast (Nilsson and Hamberger, 1994). A review for the disk in *Wired*, a prominent cyberculture magazine with about an 80 per cent male readership, assures the potential buyer, 'Interactivity remains an option, never an interruption or a chore' (Gasperini, 1994: 198). Truly, we are in the realm of miracles, beginnings and promises. A secular terrain has never been more explicitly sacred, embedded in the narratives of God's first Creation, which is repeated in miniature with each new life (Harding, 1990). Secular, scientific visual culture is in the immediate service of the narratives of Christian realism. We are in both an echo chamber and a house of mirrors, where, in word and image, ricocheting mimesis structures the emergence of subjects and objects. It does not seem too much to claim that the biomedical, public fetus – given flesh by the high technology of visualization – is a sacred–secular incarnation, the material realization of the promise of life itself. Here is the fusion of art, science and creation. No wonder we look.

The Kelly cartoon is practically an exact tracing of its original. Looking at Kelly's cartoon returns the reader of comics to Michelangelo's *Creation of Adam*. For 'modern' viewers, the entire ceiling of the Sistine Chapel signifies an eruption of salvation history into a newly powerful visual narrative medium. Accomplished between 1508 and 1512 under the patronage of Pope Julius II, the ceiling's frescos mark a technical milestone in mastering the Renaissance problem of producing a convincing pictorial rendering of narrative. The gestures and attitudes of the human body sing with stories. Part of the apparatus of production of Christian humanism, which has animated the history of western science, European early modern or Renaissance painting developed key techniques for the realization of man. Or, at least, that is a key way 'modern man' tells his history.

Although I will not trace them, innovations in literary technology are also part of this story. Eric Auerbach (1953) places the critical mutation in Dante's *Divine Comedy*, with its powerful figurations of salvation history that locate promised transcendental fulfillment in the material tissues of solid narrative flesh. Figurations are performative images that can be inhabited. Verbal or visual, figurations are condensed maps of whole worlds. In art, literature and science, my subject is the technology that turns body into story, and vice versa, producing both what can count as real and the witnesses to that reality. In my own mimetic critical method, I am tracing some of the circulations of Christian realism in the flesh of technoscience. I work to avoid the terms 'Judeo-Christian' or 'monotheist' because the dominant technoscientific visual and narrative materials here are specifically secular Christian renditions of partially shared Jewish, Muslim and Christian origin stories for science, self and world. But I am also trying to trace the story within a story, within which we learn to believe that fundamental revolutions take place. I am trying to retell some of the conditions of possibility of the stories technoscientific humans continue to tell ourselves. It is doubtful that historical configurations conventionally called the 'Renaissance', or in a later version of the birth of the modern, the 'Scientific Revolution', or today's rendition called the 'New World Order' actually have been unique, transformative theatres of origin. But they have been narrativized and canonized as such cradles of modern humanity, especially technoscientific humanity with its secular salvation and damnation histories. Certainly, if only by opposition, I am complicit in the narrativization and figuration of the Scientific Revolution and the New World Order.

Metonymic for the entire array of Renaissance visual techniques, Albrecht Dürer's *Draughtsman Drawing a Nude* (1538) conventionally dramatizes the story of a revolutionary apparatus for turning disorderly bodies into disciplined art and science. In the drawing, an old man uses a line-of-sight device and a screen-grid to transfer point-for-point the features of a voluptuous, reclining female nude onto a paper grid marked off into squares. The upright screen-grid separates the prone woman on the table, whose hand is poised over her genitals, from the erectly seated draughtsman, whose hand guides his stylus on the paper. Dürer's engraving attests to the power of the technology of perspective to discipline vision to produce a

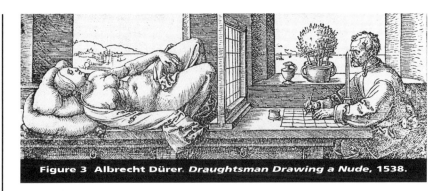

Figure 3 Albrecht Dürer. *Draughtsman Drawing a Nude*, 1538.

new kind of knowledge of form. As art historian Lynda Nead argued, '[V]isual perception is placed on the side of art and in opposition to the information yielded through tactile perception. . . . Through visual perception we may achieve the illusion of a coherent and unified self' (Nead, 1992: 28). Here also, with Dürer, the disciplining screen between art and pornography is paradigmatically erected.

The gendering of this kind of vision is, of course, not subtle. Indeed, feminists argue that this visual technology was part of the apparatus for the *production* of modern gender, with its proliferating series of sexually charged oppositions condensed into the tension at the interface between touch and vision. Nead writes, 'Woman offers herself to the controlling discipline of illusionistic art. With her bent legs closest to the screen, [Dürer's] image recalls not simply the life class but also the gynaecological examination. Art and medicine are both foregrounded here, the two discourses in which the female body is most subjected to scrutiny and assessed according to historically specific norms' (1992: 11). Obviously, it is only after the institutions of the life class and the gynaecological exam emerged that Dürer's print can be retrospectively read to recall them. As part of reforming her own self-making technology, Nead, the feminist art historian, is telling a story about the birth of the figure of Woman. As for me, the feminist analyst of technoscience attuned to artistic and biomedical visual delights, I see Dürer's majestic print and Bell Telephone's television advertising through the grid of Kelly's virtual speculum. In the life class and gynaecological exam that is technoscience, critique caresses comedy. I laugh; therefore, I am . . . implicated. I laugh; therefore, I am responsible and accountable. That is the best I can do for moral foundations at the tectonic fault line joining the sacred, the scientific and the comic. And everyone knows that end-of-the-millennium Californians build their houses, and their theories, on fault lines.

In Renaissance visual technology, form and narrative implode; and both seem merely to reveal what was already there, waiting for unveiling or discovery. This epistemology underlies the European-indebted sense of what counts as reality in the culture, believed by many of its practitioners to transcend all culture, called modern science. Reality, as westerners have known it in story and image for several hundred years, is an *effect*, but cannot be recognized as such without great moral and epistemological angst. The conjoined western modern sense of the 'real' and the 'natural' was achieved by a set of fundamental innovations in visual technology beginning in the Renaissance.[3]

Twentieth-century scientists call on this earlier visual technology for insisting on a specific kind of reality, which readily makes today's observers forget the conditions, apparatuses and histories of its production. Especially in computer and information sciences and in biotechnology and biomedicine, representations of late twentieth-century technosciences make liberal use of iconic exemplars of early modern European art/humanism/technology. Current images of technoscience quote, point to, and otherwise evoke a small, conventional, potent stock of Renaissance visual analogues, which provide a legitimate lineage and origin story for technical revolutions at the end of the Second Christian Millennium. Today's Renaissance *Sharper Image Catalogue* includes the anatomized human figures in *De humanis corporis fabrica of* Andreas Vesalius, published in Basel in 1543; Leonardo da Vinci's drawing of the human figure illustrating proportions, or the 'Vitruvian Man' (c. 1485–90); Dürer's series of plates on perspective techniques; the maps of the cartographers of the 'Age of Discovery'; and, of course, Michelangelo's *Creation of Adam*. Invoking this ready stock, a venture capitalist from Kleiner Perkins Caufield & Byers mutated the analogies to make a related historical observation, noting that biotech has been 'for human biology what the Italian Renaissance was for art' (Hamilton 1994: 85). In technoscientific culture, at the risk of mild overstatement, I think one can hardly extend an index finger (or finger substitute) toward another hand (or hand substitute) without evoking the First Author's gesture (or First Author Substitute's gesture).

In Michelangelo's version of authorship, Adam lies on the earth; and, conveyed by angels, God moves toward him from the heavens. An elderly, patriarchal God the Father reaches his right index finger to touch the languidly extended, left index finger of an almost liquid, nude, young-man Adam. A conventional art history text concludes, 'Adam, lying like a youthful river god, awakens into life' (Hays, 1967: 99; see also Jansen and Jansen 1963: 359–60). Adam is a kind of watery, earth-borne fetus of humanity, sparked into life on a new land by the heavenly Father.

FEMINIST REVIEW NO 55, SPRING 1997

Michelangelo's God, however, is also carrying another, truly unborn human being. Still in the ethereal regions above earth, Eve is held in the shelter of God's left arm; and at the origin of mankind she and Adam are looking toward each other. It is not entirely clear who Adam sees, God or Woman – exactly the problem addressed by the screen barrier between art and pornography. Maybe in innocence before the Fall and at the moment of the renaissance of modern vision, a yearning Adam can still see both at once. Touch and vision are not yet split. Adam's eye caresses both his Author and his unborn bride.

Anne Kelly's drawing suggests other screens as well, such as that between art and science, on the one hand, and caricature and politics, on the other. Like the transparent film between art and pornography, the interface between the medico-scientific image and the political cartoon unstably both joins and separates modest witnesses and contaminated spectators. In both potent zones of transformation, the reclining female nude seems suggestively common. Dürer's woman in *Draughtsman Drawing a Nude*, the *Venus d'Urbino* by Titian (1487?–1576), the *Rokeby Venus* by Diego Velázquez (1599–1660), *Venus at Her Toilet* by Peter Paul Rubens (1577–1640), and Edouard Manet's *Olympia* (1863) are all ancestors for Kelly's first woman. Kelly's cartoon figure depends on the conventions for drawing the recumbent nude female in modern western painting. Dürer's, Titian's, Velázquez's, Rubens' and Manet's nudes all figure prominently in accounts of the emergence of modern ways of seeing (Clark 1985). The relation between Manet's African serving woman and the reclining European nude also figures in the fraught racialized visual history of modern Woman (Nead, 1992: 34–46; Harvey, 1989: 54–56). Clearly, the *Virtual Speculum* keeps its eyes on the prize.

Lynn Randolph's painting, *Venus*, part of her *Ilusas* or 'deluded women' series, is a more formal feminist intervention into the conventions of the female nude and her associated secretions and tools. Scrutinizing the standard line between pornography and art, Randolph (1993: 1) writes:

> This contemporary Venus is not a Goddess in the classical sense of a contained figure. She is an unruly woman, actively making a spectacle of herself. Queering Botticelli, leaking, projecting, shooting, secreting milk, transgressing the boundaries of her body. Hundreds of years have passed and we are still engaged in a struggle for the interpretive power over our bodies in a society where they are marked as a battleground by the church and the state in legal and medical skirmishes.

Kelly, however, is drawing a female Adam, not a Venus. The story is different, and so is the optical technology. Kelly's woman looks not into the mirror that fascinates Rubens' and Velázquez' nudes, but into a screen that

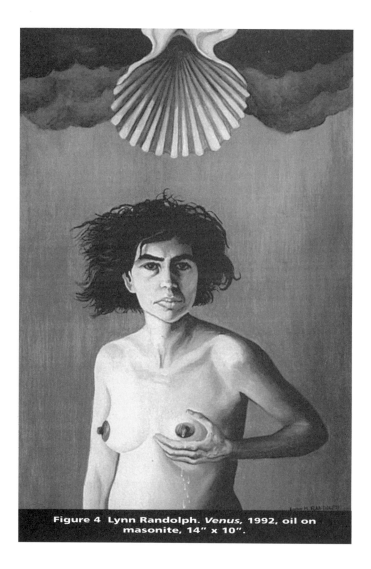

Figure 4 Lynn Randolph. *Venus,* 1992, oil on masonite, 14" x 10".

is in the heavenly position of Michelangelo's God. The 'venereal' women with mirrors in the history of western painting have given way in Kelly to the 'authorial' woman with keyboard and computer terminal. Kelly's woman is not in a story of reflections and representations. Whatever she sees, it is not her reflection. The computer screen is not a mirror; the fetus is not her double or her copy. First woman in *Virtual Speculum* looks not into the normal reality established by Renaissance perspective, but into the virtual reality given by a time called postmodernity. Both realities are technical effects of particular apparatuses of visual culture. Both realities are simultaneously material, embodied and imaginary. Both realities can only be inhabited by subjects who learn how to see and touch with the right

33

conventions. It's all a question of interactive visual technology. Reach out and touch someone; this is the long distance call.

Not under the arm of God, but in computer-generated visual space, the fetus meets first woman's gaze. Kelly's unborn fetus, not the Adam-like woman, is in the position of Michelangelo's still-uncreated Eve. From the non-perspective of virtual space, the first woman and the fetus confront each other, as Adam and Eve did in Michelangelo's version of human creation. In that reading, the computer screen is the embracing arm of God. Has His gender value been transmuted as Adam's has been? Is the computer womb now female, or is gender one of the many things at stake? Kelly's cartoon allows at least two readings of the fetus: it is either in the position of God or in that of the not-yet-created Eve. If the fetus is Eve, the computer itself, with keyboard, is the encompassing deity reaching out to the female Adam's extended but limp hand. That reading makes Kelly's Adam the effect of the computer, the effect of the 'creative' technologies of cyberspace. On the other hand, the female Adam has her hand on the keypad; she seems to be in the position of author. Then, the fetus is her file, which she is writing, editing or, as one viewer suggested, deleting. Certainly, the politics of abortion are implicitly in this cartoon. Maybe she is reaching for the 'escape' key, or perhaps merely the 'control' key.

Like traditional masculine figures in the reproductive imagery of technoscience, who have brain children all the time, Kelly's first woman seems to have a pregnancy associated with the organs of cognition and writing. Her pregnancy is literally extra-uterine. Or, perhaps Kelly's Adam is not pregnant at all; she may be viewing a fetus with no further connection to her once the file is closed. Literally, the fetus is somehow 'in' the computer. This fetus is a kind of data structure, whose likely fate seems more connected to downloading than birth or abortion. Just as the computer as womb-brain signifies the superior creativity of artificial intelligence (AI), the on-screen fetus is an artificial life (ALife) form. As such, *Virtual Speculum*'s fetus is *not* disembodied. Rather, the specific form of embodiment inside the apparatuses of technoscience is the material conundrum presented by the cartoon. The computer is metonymic for technoscience, an inescapable materialization of the world. Life itself, a kind of technoscientific deity, may be what is virtually pregnant. These ontologically confusing *bodies*, and the practices that produce specific embodiment, are what we have to address, not the false problem of *dis*embodiment. Whose and which bodies – human and non-human, silicon-based and carbon-based – are at stake and how, in our technoscientific dramas of origin? And what is the specific political and moral accountability attached to these not-always-human bodies?

The proliferating readings of Kelly's cartoon make one conclusion inescapable: reversals and substitutions never just substitute for or reverse the values of the original. Rather, reversals and substitutions undo the original, opening the story up in unexpected ways. Themselves forms of repetition, reversals and substitutions make the condition of all repetition obvious. The great stories of mimesis are undone. Caricature breaks the unspoken agreements that stabilized the original. Caricatures break the frame of salvation history. Perhaps that point gives the key for reading the multiple out-of-frame elements of Kelly's cartoon. The pregnancy is ectopic, to say the least; the fetal umbilical cord and barely visible placenta go off screen on the display terminal; and the electrical cords wander up and off screen from the whole cartoon, with no point of attachment in view. The computer terminal, itself a work station, seems to be the meta-fetus in the picture. Further, this meta-fetus is an extrauterine abortus, with ripped out umbilical cords like those in Lennart Nilsson's emblematic photographs of the beginnings of life itself. There is an odd kind of obstetrical art and technology at work here. It is not just Dürer's visual technology that makes a feminist 'recall' the gynecological exam and the life class, those troubling and productive scenes of medical science and of art. In Kelly's meditation, the examination of both art and life is distinctly eccentric.

Fetal Work Stations and Feminist Technoscience Studies

If Kelly's fetus cannot be the woman's reflection, the unborn being might be her project, or someone's project. More likely, the fetus in cyberspace signifies an entity that is constituted by many variously related communities of practice. This fetus is certainly an object of attention and a locus of work (Casper, 1995b), and Kelly's First Woman is at her workstation. Feminist scholars have also been at a 'fetal workstation'. Like data processors at their video terminals in the information economy, feminists' positions at their analytical keyboards have not always been a matter of choice. Reproduction has been at the centre of scientific, technological, political, personal religious, gender, familial, class, race and national webs of contestation for at least the last twenty-five years. Like it or not, as if we were children dealing with adults' hidden secrets, feminists could not avoid relentlessly asking where babies come from. Our answers have repeatedly challenged the reduction of that original and originating question to literalized and universalized women's body parts. It turns out that addressing the question of where babies come from puts us at the centre of the action in the New World Order. With roots in local and international women's health movements as well as in various scholarly communities, since the early 1970s feminists have developed a rich toolkit for technoscience studies through their attention to the social-technical webs that constitute reproductive practice (Ginsberg and Rapp, 1991, 1995). Idiosyncratically, I will inspect a small, recent inventory from this toolbox in order to pursue my inquiry into the optical properties of the virtual speculum.

In their powerful paper on the many constituencies who construct the French abortifacent called RU486, sociologist Adele Clarke and her former student Teresa Montini developed social worlds and arena analysis for feminist science studies. Clarke and Montini (1993) identify reproductive and other scientific-medical specialists; pharmaceutical companies; anti-abortion groups; feminist pro-choice groups; women's health movement groups; politicians, Congress, and the Food and Drug Administration; and women users and consumers of RU486. The authors are clear that their own analysis turns the volume up or down on some actors more than others; their own representations are part of the struggle for what will count as reproductive freedom, and for whom. Attention to this kind of point characterizes feminist science studies in general, whether generated from the academy or policy-forming and community-action sites.

Using these tools, Monica Casper (1995a and b) studies human fetal surgery historically and ethnographically. Casper is developing the notions of the 'technofetus' and the 'fetus as work object'. Casper's approach shows the fetus to be the site and result of multiple actors' work practices, including the mother's. Because Casper is necessarily a member of inter-digitating communities of scholarly and political practice, her own pos-itioning is neither invisible nor unaccountable. The many communities of practice who are held together around the technofetus are by no means necessarily in harmony. Their work tools – rhetorical and material – can make the fetus into very different kinds of entities. However, neither 'mul-tiplicity' nor 'contestation' for their own sake are the point in feminist science studies. Joining analysts to subjects and objects of analysis, ques-tions of power, resources, skills, suffering, hopes, meanings and lives are always at stake.

In a similar spirit, Charis Cussins (1996), trained in a science studies pro-gramme, traces the continual 'ontological choreography' that constructs subjects, objects and agents at an infertility clinic. Subjects and objects are made and unmade in many ways in the extended processes of infertility treatment. Cussins shows that the different stakes, temporalities, trajecto-ries and connections and disconnections to women's and others' bodies and part-bodies – as humans and non-humans are enrolled together in the prac-tices of technoscience – require ethnographic, sustained inquiry.

Anthropologist Rayna Rapp's multi-year ethnographic study of women in New York City from many social classes, ethnicities, language communities and racially marked groups also vividly describes the plethora of material-semiotic worlds in which fetuses and pregnant women have their being (Rapp, 1994 and forthcoming). Women who accept and who refuse the procedures of fetal genetic diagnosis, research geneticists, genetic counsellors, family members, support groups for people with genetically disabled children – all these people, variously intertwined with machines, babies, fetuses, clinical materials and with each other, make up Rapp's research community. The consequences of all the actors' locations in these dynamic, differentiated worlds are crucial to her account; and her own profound mutations in the course of doing the work grow from and feed back into the research and writing.

In the linked interdisciplinary worlds of feminist accounts of technoscience, Valerie Hartouni (1996), located professionally in a communications department, takes up the many contending discourses of maternal nature in contemporary reproductive cultures in the US. In a subtle and incisive series of essays, Hartouni examines how class, gender and genetic parenthood interdigitate in the Baby M surrogate mother legal arguments; how the judicial injunction not to speak of race in the case of the African-American gestational surrogate Anna Johnson, who carried a child for a mixed-race (Filipina-Anglo) couple, was nonetheless part of the saturation of the case with racial and class markings; and how the performance video, S'Aline's Abortion, despite explicit pro-choice intentions, nonetheless was positioned by its visual rhetoric inside anti-choice narratives for many audiences. Hartouni's work is part of the broad feminist inquiry into how the genetic relationship displaces other discourses of connection to a child in legal, biotechnical, familial and entertainment worlds. Her writing contributes to the project of crafting feminist visual literacy needed for working effectively inside a reproductive technoscience politics saturated with visual communications practices.

Reproductive politics are at the heart of questions about citizenship, liberty, family and nation. Feminist questions are not a 'special preserve', but a 'general' discourse critical for science studies as such. Inaugural acts of chief executive officers in mid-1990s US politics illustrate an aspect of this claim. After taking the oath of office as President of the United States in January 1993, Bill Clinton issued his first executive orders, which established his presidency symbolically and materially. His first acts did not concern war or other conventional domains of national interest and manly action. His first acts had to do with embryos and fetuses embedded in technoscientific contestations. Through embryos and fetuses, those orders had to do with entire forms of life – public, embodied and personal – for the citizens of the state. Clinton began the process of lifting restrictions on providing information about abortion in federally funded clinics, permitting medical experimentation on aborted fetal tissue and allowing the importation of the controversial abortifacent and potential cancer treatment, RU486.

Similarly, but with opposite political intent, the first official act of Pete Wilson after he was re-elected Governor of California in 1994 was to order a state programme closed that provided pre-natal care to pregnant 'undocumented' immigrant women. Wilson had staked his campaign on Proposition 187, which denied so-called illegal immigrants virtually all social services, especially public education and non-emergency medical care. Despite the denials of its backers, Proposition 187 was widely understood to have fundamental racial-ethnic, class and national targets, especially working-class Latinos of colour coming across the Mexican–US border. The measure passed by a two-to-one margin. That is, Proposition 187 was overwhelmingly popular with the older, Republican, white and economically affluent electorate who voted in the 1994 election – many of whom, including a candidate for US Senate who supported Proposition 187, had recently hired 'illegal' women of colour to care for their white children, while seeking to withhold social services from the children of these same employees. To withhold reproductive health care from 'undocumented' women of colour, whose children would be born US citizens if their pregnancies came to term in California, was the first concern of the re-elected executive. Fetal protection (and the health of women) suddenly looked like a bad idea, and fetal endangerment (and the endangerment of 'illegal' women of colour) was the direct implication of the governor's inaugural act. Biomedicine – where post-natal people, machines, fetuses, health beliefs, diagnostic procedures and bodily fluids are enrolled together into potent configurations – was the arena of conflict. Biomedicine is where freedom, justice and citizenship were at stake.

Finally, Clinton's first public acts as commander-in-chief threatened to queer the sacred site of the citizen-warrior by changing the US armed forces' policy of excluding acknowledged gay men and lesbians from the military. The citizen-soldier's 'manliness' has long been at the centre of the political theory of the state and citizenship. However inadequately, colour and gender were addressed in the US military before the category of queer. The tragicomic panic that ensued in Congress and among the Joint Chiefs of Staff thwarted Clinton's intent to deal with the matter by executive order. My point is that discursive, embodied entities like the fetus, the pregnant immigrant and the homosexual are not the subjects of 'social' issues, in contrast to 'political' matters of state and public policy. Like the embryo or fetus and the 'undocumented' pregnant woman, the queer is at the heart of contests to reconfigure precisely what public space is and who inhabits it. Technoscience is intrinsic to all of these struggles.

The work sketched here shows that to study technoscience requires an immersion in worldly material–semiotic practices, where the analysts, as well as the humans and non-humans studied, are all at risk – morally, politically, technically and epistemologically. Science studies that do not take on that kind of situated knowledge practice stand a good chance of floating off screen into an empyrean and academic never-never land. 'Ethnography', in this extended sense, is not so much a specific procedure in anthropology, as it is a method of being at risk in the face of the practices and discourses into which one inquires. To be at risk is not the same thing as identifying with the subjects of study; quite the contrary. And self-identity is as much at risk as the temptation to identification. One is at risk in the face of serious non-identity that challenges previous stabilities, convictions or ways of being of many kinds. An 'ethnographic attitude' can be adopted within any kind of inquiry, including textual analysis. Not limited to a specific discipline, an ethnographic attitude is a mode of practical and theoretical attention, a way of remaining mindful and accountable. Such a method is not about 'taking sides' in a pre-determined way, but neither are moral and political commitments hygienically expunged. Ethnography as I understand the practice is about risks, purposes, meanings and hopes – one's own and others' – embedded in knowledge projects, including technoscientific ones (Downey and Dumit, forthcoming; Escobar, 1994).

Ethnography is not only a mode of attention, however. Textual analysis must articulate with many kinds of sustained scholarly interaction among living people in living situations, historical and contemporary, documentary and *in vivo*. These different studies need each other, and they are all theory-building projects. No one person does all the kinds of work; feminist science studies is a collective undertaking that cultivates a practice of learning to be at risk in all the sorts of work necessary to an account of technoscience and medicine.

Under these conditions, looking for a feminist doctrine on reproductive technology, in particular, or on technoscience, in general, would be ludicrous. But understanding feminist technoscience scholarship as a contentious search for what accountability to freedom projects for women might mean, and how such meanings are crafted and sustained in a polyglot world of men and women, is not ludicrous. Pre-set certainties, feminist and otherwise, about what is happening in theatres of reproduction, or any theatre of technoscience, stand an excellent chance of being flagrantly wrong. But feminist questions shape vision-generating technologies for science studies. Freedom and justice questions are intrinsic to the inquiry about the joinings of humans and non-humans. Feminist technoscience inquiry is a speculum, a surgical instrument, a tool for widening the openings into all kinds of orifices to improve observation and intervention in the interest of projects that are simultaneously about freedom, justice and knowledge. In these terms, feminist inquiry is no more innocent, no more free of the inevitable wounding that all questioning brings, than any other knowledge project.

It does not matter much to the figure of the still-gestating, feminist, anti-racist, mutated modest witness whether freedom, justice and knowledge are branded as modernist or not; that is not our issue. We have never been modern (Latour, 1993; Haraway, 1994). Rather, freedom, justice and know-ledge are – in bell hooks' terms – about 'yearning', not about putative Enlightenment foundations. Keep your eyes on the prize. Keep our eyes on the prize. For hooks, yearning is an affective and political sensibility allow-ing cross-category ties that 'would promote the recognition of common com-mitments and serve as a base for solidarity and coalition' (hooks, 1990: 27; see also Braidotti, 1994: 1–8; and Sandoval, forthcoming). Yearning must also be seen as a cognitive sensibility. Without doubt, such yearning is rooted in a reconfigured unconscious, in mutated desire, in the practice of love, in the ecstatic hope for the corporeal and imaginary materialization of the anti-racist female subject of feminism. And all other possible subjects of femin-ism. Finally, freedom, justice and knowledge are not necessarily nice and definitely not easy. Neither vision nor touch is painless, on or off screen.

The Right Speculum for the Job[4]

An inquiry into instruments of visualization, Kelly's cartoon can carry us another step toward understanding feminist science studies. *Virtual Specu-lum* is replete with signifiers of 'choice', a term that has been encrusted by colonies of semiotic barnacles in the reproductive politics of the last quarter century. What counts as choice, for whom, and at what cost? What is the relation of 'choice' to 'life', and especially to 'life itself'?

Kelly's cartoon is not denunciatory. I do not see in it any stereotyped posi-tion on new reproductive technologies or pious certainty about supposed alienation and disembodiment. Nor is Kelly's cartoon celebratory. It does not reflect credit on the original; it does not announce a new scientific age in the image of an original Creation. The cartoon depends on signifiers of information and communications technologies. Information is a technical term for signal-to-noise discrimination; information is a statistical affair for dealing with differences. Information is not embedded in a metaphysics of reflection and representation. The pixel grid of the cartoon's screen will not yield a point-for-point emplotment of an original body, disciplined through an ontology and epistemology of mimesis, reflection and rep-resentation. Kelly is not Dürer.

Instead, *Virtual Speculum* is diffractive and interrogatory: It asks, 'Is this what feminists mean by choice, agency, life and creativity? What is at stake here, and for whom? Who and what are the human and non-human centres of action? Whose story is this? Who cares?' The view screen records interfering and shifted – diffracted – patterns of signifiers and bodies. What displacements in reproductive positioning matter to whom and why? What are the conditions of effective reproductive freedom? Why are public and personal narratives of self-creation linked to those of pregnancy? Whose stories are these? Who is in the cartoon, who is missing, and so what? What does it mean to have the public fetus on screen? Whose fetuses merit such extraordinary attention? What does it mean to embed a joke about self-creation and pregnancy inside western and 'white' conventions for painting the female nude? Kelly's cartoon is embedded inside signifiers of the Creation, Renaissance, Scientific Revolution, Information Age and New World Order. How does salvation history get replicated or displaced inside technoscience? What are the consequences of the overwhelmingly Christian signifiers of technoscience? If Michel Foucault wrote about the care of the self and the development of disciplinary knowledge in two different cultural configurations within western history, Kelly is sketching an inquiry into the apotheosis of the fetus and reproductive technoscience as a diagnostic sign of the end of the Second Christian Millennium. How is care of the fetus today analogous to care of the self in classical antiquity – an elite set of practices for producing certain kinds of subjects?

What is the right speculum for the job of opening up observation into the orifices of the technoscientific body politic to address these kinds of questions about knowledge projects? I want to approach that question by going back to the eruption of the gynaecological speculum as a symbol in US feminist politics in the early 1970s. Many feminists of my cohorts – largely young, white, middle-class women – 'seized the masters' tools' in the context of the Women's Liberation Movement and its activist women's health movement (Lorde, 1984). Armed with a gynaecological speculum, a mirror, a flashlight and – most of all – each other in a consciousness-raising group, women ritually opened their bodies to their own literal view. The speculum had become the symbol of the displacement of the female midwife by the specialist male physician and gynaecologist. The mirror was the symbol forced on women as a signifier of our own bodies as spectacle-for-another in the guise of our own supposed narcissism. Vision itself seemed to be the empowering act of conquerors.

More than a little amnesiac about how colonial travel narratives work, we peered inside our vaginas toward the distant cervix and said something like, 'Land ho! We have discovered ourselves and claim the new territory for women.' In the context of the history of western sexual politics – that is, in the context of the whole orthodox history of western philosophy and technology – visually self-possessed sexual and generative organs made potent tropes for the reclaimed feminist self. We thought we had our eyes on the prize. I am caricaturing, of course, but with a purpose. 'Our Bodies, Ourselves' was both a popular slogan and the title of a landmark publication in women's health movements.[5]

The repossessed speculum, sign of the Women's Liberation Movement's attention to material instruments in science and technology, was understood to be a self-defining technology. Those collective sessions with the speculum and mirror were not only symbols, however. They were self-help and self-experimentation practices in a period in which abortion was still illegal and unsafe. The self-help groups developed techniques of menstrual extraction, i.e., early abortion, that could be practised by women alone or with each other outside professional medical control. A little flexible tubing joined the mirror and the speculum in more than a few of those sessions. Meanwhile, biomedical clinicians were introducing the sonogram and endoscopic fetal visualization, while Lennart Nilsson's photographs spread around the medicalized globe. We had to wonder early if we had seized the right tools.

Still, the sense of empowerment experienced by the women in early 1970s self-help groups was bracing. The spirit was captured in a cartoon in the July 1973 issue of *Sister,* the Newspaper of the Los Angeles Women's Center. Wonder Woman – the Amazonian princess from Paradise Isle, complete with her steel bracelets that could deter bullets; stiletto high heels; low-cut, eagle-crested bodice; star-spangled, blue mini-shorts; and her magic lasso for capturing evil doers and other transportation needs – seizes the radiant speculum from the white-coat-clad, stethoscope-wearing, but cowering white doctor and announces, 'With my speculum, I **am** strong! I **can** fight!'

Wonder Woman entered the world in 1941 in Charles Moulton's popular cartoon strips. Moulton was William Moulton Marston, psychologist, attorney, inventor of the lie-detector test, prison reformer and businessman. Marston's conventional feminism ascribed force bound by love to women and opposed that to men's attraction to force alone. Despite her origins in the Amazon, Wonder Woman's ethnicity was unmistakably white. Her expletives ('Merciful Minerva!' and 'Great Hera!') and her other cultural accoutrements locate her firmly in the modern myth of western origins in ancient Greece, relocated to the New World. She could have easily joined a US white sorority in the 1940s and 1950s, with their Greek-revivalist themes and rituals. The guiding goddesses of Wonder Woman's Amazonian matriarchal paradise were Aphrodite and Athena (Edgar, 1972).

Figure 5 Speculum-wielding Wonder Woman, *Sister*, newspaper of the Los Angeles Women's Center, July 1973.

After falling into a sad state by the end of the 1960s, Wonder Woman was resurrected in several venues in the early 1970s. Wonder Woman's first female comic-book editor, Dorothy Woolfolk, brought her back to the mass market in 1973. *Ms.* magazine put Wonder Woman on the cover of its first issue in July 1972, under the slogan, 'Wonder Woman for President'. The Vietnam War was raging on one side of the cover, and a 'Peace and Justice in '72' billboard adorned the store-fronts on a US street on the other side. A gigantic Wonder Woman was grabbing a US fighter jet out of the sky with one hand and carrying an enlightened city in her magic lasso in the other hand. The city might be a feminist prototype for the mass-market, computer-simulation game of the 1990s, SimCity2000™ (Bleecker, 1995). Wonder Woman's lasso outlined a glowing urban tetra-hedron that would have made Buckminster Fuller proud.

Figure 6 **Wonder Woman for President**, *Ms.*, **July 1972.**

In their ground-breaking 1973 pamphlet on medicine and politics, feminist academic and activist historians Barbara Ehrenreich and Deirdre English reprinted the *Sister* Wonder Woman figure seizing the speculum. The context was the chapter on the future, in which the authors emphasized that

> [s]elf help is not an alternative to confronting the medical system with the demands for reform of existing institutions. Self help, or more generally, self-knowledge, is critical to that confrontation. Health is an issue which has the potential to cut across class and race lines. . . . The growth of feminist

consciousness gives us the possibility, for the first time, of a truly egalitarian, mass women's health movement.

(Ehrenreich and English, 1973: 84–5)

Ehrenreich and English emphasized that not all women had the same histories or needs in the medical system.

For black women, medical racism often overshadows medical sexism. For poor women of all ethnic groups, the problem of how to get services of any kind often overshadows all qualitative concerns. . . . A movement that recognizes our biological similarity but denies the diversity of our priorities cannot be a women's health movement, it can only be *some women's* health movement.

(Ehrenreich and English, 1973: 86, italics in original)

The speculum was not a reductionist symbolic and material tool that limited the feminist health movement to the politics of 'choice' defined by demands for legal, safe abortion and attention to the new reproductive technologies. Nor was the speculum definitive of an exclusivist, middle-class, white movement. The women's health movement was actively built, and often pioneered, by women of colour and their specific organizations, as well as by mixed and largely white groups that cut across class lines.[6] That legacy is too often forgotten in the terrible history of racism, class-blindness, generational arrogance and fragmentation in American feminism, as well as in other sectors of US progressive politics. However, the fullest meanings of reproductive freedom critical to feminist technoscience politics cannot easily be signified by the gynaecological speculum, nor by the speculum of the computer terminal, no matter how important it remains to control, inhabit and shape those tools, both semiotically and materially. The loose configurations of millionaires and billionaires from Paul Simon's song at the head of this essay still determines the nature of the US health system, including reproductive health, for everybody. The structure and consequences of that complex determination are what we must learn to see if 'choice' is to have a robust meaning. The last verse of Simon's 'The Boy in the Bubble' reminds us that the relentless bursts of 'information' – in transnational and rural jungles – are a long-distance call we cannot ignore.

The Statistics of Freedom Projects

A speculum does not have to be a literal physical tool for prying open tight orifices; it can be any instrument for rendering a part accessible to observation. So, I will turn to another kind of speculum – statistical analysis coupled with freedom- and justice-oriented policy formation – to find a sharper focus for describing what feminists must mean by reproductive

FEMINIST REVIEW NO 55, SPRING 1997

freedom, in particular, and technoscientific liberty, in general. In this paper, in relation to the goals of feminist technoscience studies, I have adopted the civil rights rallying cry, 'Keep your eyes on the prize!' I mean my appropriation of this phrase to emphasize that conducting an analysis of reproductive freedom from the point of view of *marked* groups – groups that do not fit the white, or middle-class, or other 'unmarked' standard – is the only way to produce anything like a *general* statement that can bind us together as a people. Working uncritically from the viewpoint of the 'standard' groups is the best way to come up with a particularly parochial and limited analysis of technoscientific knowledge or policy, which then masquerades as a general account that stands a good chance of reinforcing unequal privilege. However, there is rarely only one kind of standard and one kind of relative marginality operating at the same time. Groups that do not fit one kind of standard can be the unmarked, standard or dominant group in another respect. Also, reproductive freedom is only one piece of what feminist technoscientific liberty must include, for women and men. Feminist technoscience studies are about much more than reproductive and health matters. Feminist technoscience studies are about technoscience *in general*. But, fundamentally, there is no way to make a *general* argument outside the never-finished work of articulating the partial worlds of *situated* knowledges. Feminism is not defined by the baby-making capacity of women's bodies; but working from that capacity, in all of its power-differentiated and culturally polyglot forms, is *one* critical link in the articulations necessary for forging freedom and knowledge projects inside technoscience.

The Associate Counsel and Director of the Black Women's Employment Program of the NAACP Legal Defense and Educational Fund (LDF), Charlotte Rutherford (1992) provides the needed perspective. A civil rights lawyer, feminist, African-American woman and mother, Rutherford articulates what reproductive freedom must mean and shows how both women's groups and civil rights organizations would have to change their priorities in order to take such freedom into account. Her argument is the fruit of intensive meetings with many African-American women's groups and of internal debate in the LDF in 1989–90 on Black women's reproductive health and the US Supreme Court rulings on abortion restrictions. A group of nationally prominent African-American women active in public policy issues 'maintained that reproductive freedoms are civil rights issues for African American women' (Rutherford, 1992: 257). From that perspective, I maintain, reproductive freedom *in general* has a much sharper resolution.

Included in the LDF formulation of reproductive freedoms for poor women were, at a minimum,

1) access to reproductive health care; 2) access to early diagnosis and proper treatment for AIDS, sexually transmitted diseases, and various cancers; 3) access to prenatal care, including drug treatment programs for pregnant and parenting drug abusers; 4) access to appropriate contraceptives; 5) access to infertility services; 6) freedom from coerced or ill-informed consent to sterilization; 7) economic security, which could prevent possible exploitation of the poor with surrogacy contracts; 8) freedom from toxics in the workplace; 9) healthy nutrition and living space; and 10) the right to safe, legal, and affordable abortion services.

(Rutherford, 1992: 257–58)

It seems to me that all the citizens would be better served by such a policy than from an approach to reproductive choice or rights that begins and ends in the well-insured, sonographically monitored, Bell Telephone system-nurtured uterus with its public fetus.

Not all African-American women are poor, and not all poor women are African-American, to put it mildly. And *all* the categories are discursively constituted and non-innocently deployed, both by those who inhabit them (by choice, coercion, inheritance or chance) and those who do not (by choice, coercion, inheritance or chance). I believe that *learning* to think about and yearn toward reproductive freedom from the *analytical and imaginative standpoint* of 'African-American women in poverty' – a ferociously lived discursive category to which I do not have 'personal' access – illuminates the general conditions of such freedom. A standpoint is not an empiricist appeal to or by 'the oppressed', but a cognitive, psychological and political tool for more adequate knowledge judged by the non-essentialist, historically contingent, situated standards of strong objectivity. Such a standpoint is the always fraught but necessary fruit of the *practice* of oppositional and differential consciousness. A feminist standpoint is a practical technology rooted in yearning, not an abstract philosophical foundation.[7]

Therefore, feminist knowledge is rooted in imaginative connection and hard-won, practical coalition – which is not the same thing as identity, but does demand self-critical situatedness and historical seriousness. Situatedness does not mean parochialism or localism; but it does mean specificity and consequential, if variously mobile, embodiment. Connection and coalition are bound to sometimes painful structures of accountability to each other and to the worldly hope for freedom and justice.[8] If they are not so bound, connection and coalition disintegrate in orgies of moralism. In the kind of feminist standpoint remembered and put back to work in this essay, much important feminist knowledge must be technically 'impersonal'. Statistics have an important but fraught history in the crafting of

FEMINIST REVIEW NO 55, SPRING 1997

authoritative, impersonal knowledge in democratic societies. The history of statistics is directly related to the ideals of objectivity and democracy.

In Theodore Porter's terms (1994, 1995), statistics is a basic technology for crafting objectivity and stabilizing facts. Objectivity is less about realism than it is about intersubjectivity. The impersonality of statistics is one aspect of the complex intersubjectivity of objectivity; i.e., of the public quality of technoscientific knowledge. Feminists have high stakes in the speculum of statistical knowledge for opening up otherwise invisible, singular experience to reconfigure public, widely lived reality. Credible statistical representation is one aspect of building connection and coalition that has nothing to do with moralistic 'standing in the place of the oppressed' by some act of imperialistic fantasy or with other caricatures of feminist intersubjectivity and feminist standpoint. Demanding the competent staffing and funding of the bureaus that produce reliable statistics, producing statistical representations in our own institutions, and contesting for the interpretation of statistics are indispensable to feminist technoscientific politics. Providing powerful statistical data is essential to effective public representations of what feminist and other progressive freedom and justice projects mean.[9] Recording, structuring, processing and articulating such data should raise at least as interesting scientific problems as any that have merited a Nobel Prize in economics so far.

Porter argued that 'it is precisely the communicability of numbers and of these rules [for manipulating numbers] that constitutes their claim to objectivity. . . . The crucial insight here is to see objectivity as a way of forming ties across wide distances' (1994: 48). Porter believed that this kind of objectivity inheres in specialist communities, which rely on expertise rather than on community and which substitute quantitative representations for trust and face-to-face interactions. He sees such modes of objectivity to be ill-adapted to express moral and ethical arguments (1994: 49). However, I believe that the history of struggle to recraft and stabilize public realities as part of learning to put together general policies from the analytical, imaginative and embodied standpoint of those who inhabit too many zones of unfreedom and yearn toward a more just world shows 'impersonal', quantitative knowledge to be a vital dimension of moral, political and personal reflection and action.

Crafting a politics that refuses the constrictions of both the abortion and new reproductive technology debates, with their inadequate discourse of choice, Charlotte Rutherford explores the requirements for reproductive freedom by means of statistical illustrations of the differential conditions that are experienced by women differently marked by race and class in the US. For example, in 1990, '29.3% of all African American families had incomes below the poverty level, compared to 8.1% of white families and 10.7% of families of all races'. In 1985, because of the confluence of medically uninsured women's situations and the fact that 80 per cent of private insurance policies did not include office visits or services for preventive care, 'at least 76% of all women of reproductive age must pay themselves for preventive, non-surgical reproductive health care'. The maternal mortality rate (the number of deaths of mothers per 100,000 live births) for all African-American women in 1986 was 19.3 compared to 4.7 for white mothers. 'In 1986, African American women were 3.8 times more likely than white women to die from pregnancy-related causes.' 'Blacks were more than twice as likely as whites to have late (third trimester) or no prenatal care . . . and the frequency of late or no care among American Indians was at least as high as that for Blacks.'

'In 1991, almost five million working mothers maintained their families alone and 22.3% of them lived in poverty. . . . In 1988, of all poor African American families, 75.6% were maintained by African American women alone, compared to 44% of poor white families and 47.8% of poor Hispanic families.' '[I]n 1987, only 18% of the pregnancies to women under age 20 resulted in births that were intended, while 40% resulted in births that were not intended, and 42% ended in abortion.' 'Among households headed by individuals between 15 and 24 years of age, the poverty rate is staggering: 65.3% for young African American families and 28.5% for young white families.' 'The risk of infertility is one and a half times greater for African Americans [23% of couples] than for whites [15% of couples].' 'Whites and those with higher incomes are more likely to pursue infertility treatment than are African Americans and the poor.' 'About 75% of low-income women in need of infertility services have not received any services. . . . Among all higher income women, 47% [in need of them] have received no services.' Among physicians who provide infertility services in the US, only 21% accept Medicaid patients for such care. 'By 1982, only fifteen percent of white women were sterilized, compared to twenty-four percent of African American women, thirty-five percent of Puerto Rican women, and forty-two percent of Native American women. Among Hispanic women living in the Northeast, sterilization rates as high as sixty-five percent have been reported.' Still in the 1990s, the federal government will pay for sterilization for poor women, but not abortions. The worst sterilization abuses of the recent past have been reduced by consent forms and procedures put in place since the 1970s, but the conditions leading poor women to 'choose' sterilization more often because other options are worse are not acceptable. Meanwhile, 'in 1985 eighty-two percent of all counties in the United States – home to almost one-third of the women of reproductive age – had no abortion provider.' To say the least, the situation has not improved in the 1990s. Restrictions on poor women's access to abortion mean later abortions. 'In 1982, after the ban on federal funding was implemented, 50% of Medicaid-eligible patients had their abortions after nine weeks of pregnancy, compared with only 37% of non-Medicaid-eligible women.'[10]

Rutherford also shows that toxins and other hazards in neighborhoods and workplaces differentially damage poor people and people of colour because they get more intensive and long-term exposures. To be a house-worker or janitor, hospital worker, farm worker, dry-cleaning or laundry employee, chicken processor, tobacco worker or fabric mill worker is to experience a life-time of toxic exposure that can damage reproductive cells and fetuses, not to mention adult bodily tissues. Pesticides, heat, noise, dust, mechanical hazards, poor nutrition, inadequate medical care, and high levels of stress lower life expectancies of adults, children and fetuses. Those predominantly female occupations held disproportionately by women of colour are especially dangerous to fetal and maternal health. The only thing that might be even more damaging to freedom and health is unemployment. Is anyone really surprised? 'Who cares?' is the funda-mental question for technoscientific liberty and science studies. Toxins are a civil rights issue, a reproductive freedom concern, and a feminist techno-science matter; that is, toxins are a *general* issue for technoscientific know-ledge and freedom projects.

The age of designer fetuses on screen is also the age of sharp disparities in reproductive health, and therefore of sharp disparities in technoscien-tific liberty. In the 1990s, fetuses are objects of public obsession. It is almost impossible to get through the day near the end of the Second Christian Millennium in the United States without being in communi-cation with the public fetus. As Paul Simon sang, these are the days of marvels, when the ubiquitous camera tracks the way we look to distant galaxies. The fetus hurtling through space at the end of the movie *2001* is not a feminist image; neither is the long-distance touch of Bell Tele-phone. In alliance with the women meeting with Charlotte Rutherford at the Legal Defense and Educational Fund, both Kelly's First Woman with her finger on the divine keyboard and *Sister*'s Wonder Woman seizing the gynaecological speculum must work to make the general community of women publicly visible as movers and shakers in technoscience. That much, at least, is owed to the people who taught us all to keep our eyes on the prize. 'With my speculum, I **am** strong! I **can** fight!' There is still a chance, barely, to build a truly comprehensive feminist technoscience politics.

The Invisible Fetus

> [T]here are many lives and even more deaths to keep track of, numbering the bones of a people whom the state hardly thinks worth counting at all.
>
> Nancy Scheper-Hughes (1992: 30)

It seems fitting to close this meditation on the virtual speculum with an image that is not there – with the *missing* representations of fetuses and babies that must trouble anyone yearning for reproductive freedom. In a world replete with images and representations, whom can we not see or grasp, and what are the consequences of such selective blindness? From the point of view of a barely imaginable, desperately needed, transnational, intercultural and resolutely situated feminism – a feminism circulating in networks at least as disseminated, differentiated and resilient as those of flexible capitalisms's New World Order, Inc. – questions about optics are inescapable. How is visibility possible? For whom, by whom, to whom and of whom? What remains invisible, to whom and why? For those peoples who are excluded from the visualizing apparatuses of the disciplinary regimes of modern power-knowledge networks, the *averted gaze* can be as deadly as the all-seeing panopticon that surveys the subjects of the biopolitical state. Moreover, counting and visualizing are also essential to freedom projects. Not counting and not looking, for example in health and well being, can kill in the New World Order as surely as the avid seminal gaze of state curiosity, for example, in the fixing of the criminal or the addict. Similarly, the assumed naturalness of ways of living and dying can be as intolerable as the monomaniacal construction and production of all the world as technical artifact. By now, we should all know that both naturalization and technicization are equally necessary to the regimes of flexible accumulation.

Because my last image springs from a missing gaze, I have no picture to print, no publishing permission to seek. In the demographers' language, this non-image is of human 'reproductive wastage'; *i.e.*, of the dead babies and fetuses, the *missing* offspring, who populate the earth's off-screen worlds in unimaginable numbers in the late twentieth century. These are fully 'modern' or 'postmodern' fetuses and babies, brought into invisible existence within the same New World Order that ordains bright lights, genetic gymnastics and cybernetic wonders for the public fetuses of the better-off citizens of planet earth at the end of the Second Christian Millennium. These missing fetuses and babies are not residues from some sad traditional past that can be scrubbed clean by the new brooms of modernity and its sequelae in postmodernity's regimes of flexible accumulation. Quite the contrary, the missing images, and what they represent, are precisely contemporary with and embedded in the same networks as the all-too-visible, on-screen fetal data structures. If Anne Kelly's on-line fetus is postmodern, so is the uncounted fetus I am seeking in this essay. And vice versa, if 'we' have never been modern, neither have 'they' (Latour, 1993). I continue to use the flawed, deceptive terms 'modern' and 'post-modern' partly to highlight the narratives about time in which we all still generally work and partly to insist on the dispersed, powerful, practical networks of technoscience that have changed life and death on this planet, but not in the ways most accounts of either progress or declension would have it. 'Modern' and its variants should never be taken at face value. I try to force the words – like all meaning-making tools – to stumble, make a lot of racket, and generally resist naturalization. Temporality takes many shapes in the wormholes of technoscience; but the least believable figures are the divisions of the world and its inhabitants into modern and pre-modern, progressive and traditional, and similar conventions. The solid geometry of historical time is much more troubling than that.

Of course, images of hungry babies and children, if not fetuses, periodi-cally fill our television screens. It is the *mode* of presence and absence that changes for differently positioned citizens in technoscientific public repro-ductive visual culture, more than absolute presence or absence. The visual icons of hungry infants do not perform the same semiotic work as the icons of the highly cultivated, on-screen fetuses favored by Bell Telephone. Here, I want to explore one form of off-screen, out-of-frame positioning for the children of contemporary, expanding, marginalized populations.

Nancy Scheper-Hughes is responsible for my missing visual text, as I follow her through her search in the municipal records offices and *favelas* or slums of a town in a sugar-plantation region of the Brazilian *Nordeste* over the last twenty-five years. Besides drastically reducing the complexity of accounts in her book, my sketch adds analogies, renarrativizes, and uses parts of her story in ways she did not. But we are enmeshed together in webs spun by yearning and analysis.

Developing John Berger's image, Scheper-Hughes, an anthropologist, saw herself as a 'clerk or keeper of the records' – listening, watching, and recording those events and entities that the powerful do not want to know about (Scheper-Hughes, 1992: 29). The author was tracking births and deaths that still escaped the net of official national or international statis-tics late in the twentieth century. Scheper-Hughes pointed out that the sta-tistic for infant mortality was first devised in Britain 1875. The British Registration Act of 1834 required that all deaths be recorded and given a medical cause, thus replacing the 'natural deaths' of children and the aged, at least in the intentions of the reformers. Pediatrics emerged as a medical specialty in western medicine in the first decades of the twentieth century. Relative to other discourses critical to the regimes of biopower, child survival, much less fetal and infant survival, has a late pedigree everywhere as a problem requiring statistical documentation and action. Childhood malnutrition was first designated a pediatric disease with names in 1933 in the context of colonial medicine. 'Protein-calorie malnutrition in children (of which there was an epidemic in nineteenth-century England) . . . only entered medical nosology when British doctors working in the colonies discovered it as a "tropical" disease' (Scheper-Hughes, 1992: 274–5).

For Scheper-Hughes, recording was a work of recognition and an act of solidarity. She attempted to count, to make statistically visible, the reproductive history, and especially the dead babies, of the poorest women in the Brazilian town. Moreover, she linked the existence and numbers of those dead babies to precisely the same global/local developments that led their richer sisters, living in the neighborhoods in which many of the impoverished *favela* women worked as domestics, to seek the latest in prenatal care and reproductive medicine. Under-counted and on-screen: those were the two states of being under examination.

Actually, for the middle- and upper-class Brazilian women in this town, modern scientific birth meant delivery by Cesarean section, rather than the 'new reproductive technologies' favored by their northern sisters. Scheper-Hughes recounted watching young girls play at giving birth by enacting the imagined surgical scenario. After the successful play-birth, the new 'infant was immediately put on intravenous feedings!' (Scheper-Hughes, 1992: 329). Regional newspapers reported that Cesarean section delivery rates among private maternity patients in northeastern Brazil approach 70 percent.

Caught in a nightmare, I am forced to remember another context in which offspring are counted in the regimes of technoscience. An equation in theoretical population biology has two variable quantities, r and K, which can be linked to different reproductive 'strategies' adopted by species in the context of the theory of natural selection (MacArthur, 1962). 'K-selected species' are said to 'invest' tremendous resources in each individual offspring and to have rather few offspring over their lives. Each offspring, then, is a valued 'reproductive investment', in the ordinary but nonetheless stupefying languages of investment-portfolio management in which Darwin's theory has been developed in this century. On the other hand, 'r-selected species' are said to adopt the strategy of spewing as many offspring into the world as possible, with little physiological or biosocial investment in any individual, in the hope that some offspring will survive to reproduce. For biologists, all human beings, with their large and

FEMINIST REVIEW NO 55, SPRING 1997

expensive fetuses and infants, who take many years to mature to reproductive age, are paradigmatic K-selected organisms. Dandelions or cock-
roaches, with their abundant offspring, none of whom get many nutritious
goodies packed into their embryos or much parental attention during
development, are typical r-selected creatures. Low infant mortality is the
norm for K-strategists; high infant mortality is the normal state of affairs
for r-strategists. As the sociobiological authors Martin Daly and Margo
Wilson (1978: 124) put it, the contrast is between 'profligacy or careful
nurture'.[11] The mathematical equation need not carry the ideological
interpretation that seems to proliferate so readily in the texts of some socio-
biologists; but the interpretation is, so to speak, a natural one. Careful
parents with solid family values versus vermin and weeds: that seems to be
the gist of the story in Daly and Wilson's reading of an equation. I translate this lesson in evolutionary theory into human reproductive politics in
the New World Order: intensely cultivated fetuses, located at the centre of
national culture and portrayed as individuals from fertilization on, *versus*
throw-away fetuses and dead babies, located 'down there' and known only
as 'angels'.

In the US imperialist imaginary, societies 'down there' relative to the United
States, in the warm and sordid regions of the planet, seem to have lots of
human beings who act like r-strategists. The colder, more cerebral, less
genital climes to the north – if one discounts immigrants of colour and
other non-progressive types common in racist imagery – are replete with
good K-strategists. The blunt racist imagery of the warm, sordid, genital,
fecund and coloured tropics contrasted to the cold, hygienic, cerebral,
reproductively conservative and white north is officially disavowed and
discredited; but I believe it still haunts US popular and technical discourse
on many levels and on many occasions, including elections and periods of
white middle-class frenzy about 'welfare mothers'.

Scheper-Hughes estimated that the shantytown women she worked with,
or for whom she could get records, had about *six* more pregnancies than
their wealthier townswomen living nearby, but ended up with only *one*
more living child. In her ethnographic account, poorer women, especially
in younger cohorts, expressed a preference for fewer children than did
more affluent women, not more. These preferences were not realizable in
the semiotic and material conditions that the women experienced.

Simultaneously, the supposedly natural craving for a healthy child genetically related to the parents, which is said to drive reproductive heroics in contemporary wealthy nations or parts of town, seems to be a bad joke about
K-selection. The fetus – and the child tied into lucrative markets of all kinds
– becomes so important that media conglomerates and biomedical

industries, who have much more money than mothers and fathers, seem to be the major reproductive investors. Meanwhile, literally many hundreds of millions of children experience serious deprivation, including 15 million hungry children in the United States in the mid-1990s. 'In the U.S., 30 million people suffer chronic under-consumption of adequate nutrients. Almost half of the hungry are children . . . 76% of the hungry are people of color' (Allen, 1994: 2). In October, 1994, in race-undifferentiated figures, the US Census Bureau reported that 15 percent of the population, i.e., 39.3 million people, officially lived in poverty in 1993. That year, the federal government defined poverty as a family of four with a total annual income of $14,800 or less. The US child-poverty rate is about double that of any other industrialized nation. Thus, the stereotypical rich people's lament that the poor have too many children is an even worse joke about r-selection. There is too much hunger, and hunger of too many types, independently of whether there are too many children of the rich or of the poor.

I strongly believe that there are too many people on earth, not just millions, but billions, too many for long-term survival of ourselves and incomprehensible numbers of other species. That belief in no way softens questions of justice and freedom about who survives and reproduces and how. The individual human beings matter; the communities matter. Counting matters. Further, reducing population growth rates and absolute numbers in every class, race, ethnicity and other category on earth will not necessarily reduce habitat destruction, urban or rural poverty, pollution, hunger, crime, agricultural land devastation, overcrowding, unemployment, or most other evils. Population levels are not causes in such a simple sense. The story of inter-relationship is much more complex, and it is hotly contested. I am convinced that the success of comprehensive freedom and justice projects would do a much better job of alleviating suffering and reducing resource and habitat devastation than population limitation policies in the absence of such commitments. Those statements are also beliefs, ones deeply enmeshed in the fraught worlds of technoscience.

On the one hand, it seems that demographers and population specialists of every stripe do nothing but count human beings. United Nations reports, World Bank studies, national censuses and innumerable reference works are full of data about population and reproduction for every spot on earth. On the other hand, a clerk of the records – working out of the traditions of Catholic liberation theology, socialist feminism, medical anthropology and risk-taking ethnography – was still needed to count missing children in the biopolitical age. In a time of crushing overpopulation, the perverse fact is that there are *too few* living babies among the poorest residents on earth, too few in a sense that matters to thinking about technoscience studies and reproductive freedom. These missing and dead babies are, of course, intrinsic to the on-going production of overpopulation. The surplus death of the children of the poor is closer to a cause of overpopulation than one is likely to find by many other routes of analysis. The 1994 United Nations meetings on population and development in Cairo prominently advanced this proposition. Getting a grip on the motor of this surplus death is a problem of world-historical proportions. Wherever else this problem leads, it should take us to the centre of feminist technoscience studies.

To pursue these claims, let us turn back to Nancy Scheper-Hughes' story. A US white citizen, she first went to the *favelas* of the *Nordeste* of Brazil in 1964 as an idealistic 20-year-old public health and community develop-ment worker. In those years, she came to know many women of a par-ticular community, and she got involved in community-action programmes for childcare and child health. Between 1982 and 1989, after an absence of fifteen years, Scheper-Hughes returned four times to the same com-munity, this time as an anthropologist, an identity she had earlier dis-dained. The turbulent political and economic contexts of Brazil throughout those years were never far from the surface. In oral interviews and less formal interactions, Scheper-Hughes listened to the women living in this particular shantytown as they recounted reproductive histories and their meanings. She also haunted the records offices of the municipality and of hospitals, forcing recalcitrant institutions and bureaucrats to disgorge data on births and child deaths. Trying to get a grip on how many of which classes died in a year, she talked with the municipal carpenter, whose main job seemed to be making coffins for the children of the poor. His requisi-tions for the materials needed to make the boxes for dead 'angels' gave her more numbers for her growing numerical testimony.

Scheper-Hughes' figures covered several years and allowed some sense of the trajectory of infant and child death and of the reproductive histories of women of different generations. Besides combing local, regional and national data sources, Scheper-Hughes talked to pharmacists, grocers, priests and anybody else who could cast some light on her questions about birth, life and death among the very young and very poor. She talked to the better-off citizens and prowled through data on them, getting a grip on their different reproductive experiences. Across the period of her study, laws and practices governing registration of births and deaths changed sub-stantially. There is no illusion of comprehensive data in Scheper-Hughes' accounting, but there is nonetheless an arresting ethnographic picture of infant birth and death in the flexible matrices of the New World Order.

There is nothing particularly modern about high rates of birth and infant and child mortality for our species. The opposite is supposed to be the case. The orthodox story of modernity has it that a demographic transition occurs more or less reliably with modern economic development, such that both death rates and birth rates decline, albeit rarely if ever in a neatly coordinated fashion. 'Rates' themselves are a particularly modern sort of discursive object; knowledge about progress is inconceivable, literally, without knowledge of rates of change. Death rates go down first, followed at variously unfortunate intervals by birth rates. But, whatever the fits and starts of different rates for births and deaths, modernity brings in its wake a greatly lowered rate of infant and child death as a fundamental part of the demographic transition to stable populations and low birth rates.

The people among whom Nancy Scheper-Hughes studied, however, experienced quite another sort of demographic transition. Scheper-Hughes called the pattern the 'modernization of child mortality' and the 'routinization of infant death' (1992: 268–339). Scheper-Hughes emphasized the moral, social and emotional relations of mothers and whole communities to the extreme levels of infant death among them. Scheper-Hughes' descriptions and interpretations of parental reactions to child morbidity and mortality in the impoverished Brazilian *Nordeste* are controversial (e.g., Nations and Rebhun, 1988). But the descriptions of malnutrition and infant mortality are not disputed. Brazil has the eighth largest economy in the world, but about 75 percent of its citizens in the *Nordeste* are malnourished.

Riveted by the form of modernity and postmodernity Scheper-Hughes describes, I highlight here only a limited part of her story. Over the period of the study, death rates for children over a year old did decline among the very poor, as well as among the better-off. Childhood infectious disease, the traditional 'non-modern' killer of the young, was reduced by immunization. Immunization was not the only way that contemporary allopathic medicine marked the bodies of the extremely poor. In contrast to the infants and children of the rich, the poorest babies also ate a steady diet of strong antibiotics and many other types of medicine. In this context, the marginalized poor might say, 'We have never *not* been modern.' And death rates among children less than a year old went up; and the killer – drastic under-nourishment, resulting in diarrhea and death from acute dehydration – was highly modern. The modernization of child mortality meant 'the standardization of child death within the first twelve months of life and its containment to the poorest and marginalized social classes' (Scheper-Hughes, 1992: 296). By 1989, in the town Scheper-Hughes studied, 96 percent of all child deaths occurred in the first year of life.

In one sense, the cause of the increase in infant mortality seems obvious and easily remediable – loss of the practice of breast feeding. Restore the practice of breast feeding, which has continued to decrease in each generation in the 'developing world' since about 1960, and the very poor will not see their infants die in such vast numbers. Promote breast feeding, get the artificial infant-formula makers to cooperate, teach rehydration therapy, and watch death rates come down. Get poor women to 'choose' breast feeding as their grandmothers once did. These are neither new observations nor obscure solutions, and many people work hard to put them into action.

But Scheper-Hughes argues that the modernization of infant death through starvation and dehydration is *intrinsic* to the form of development practised in the Third World under the terms set by unleashed national and transnational market forces and structural adjustment policies enforced by world sources of capital. The drastically marginalized populations that teem all over the earth, including in US cities, are the direct result of up-to-the-minute (post)modernization policies over the last thirty years, and especially the last fifteen years. In the current, acute, global forms of dependent capitalism, 'marginalized' means anything but 'rare'. For Brazil, Scheper-Hughes narrates the complex patterns of the Economic Miracle, World Bank versions of economic development in the 1980s, practices of structural adjustment, inflation and the resulting falling real wage of the poorest classes. In the years following the military junta in Brazil in 1964, total national wealth increased in the context of the systematic relocation of wealth from the bottom 40 percent of the population to the top 10 percent. Progressively, in the context of mass dislocations and migrations, semi-subsistence peasants have become urban, temporary, day-wage workers in large numbers. Food has become a commodity everywhere and for everyone – including the newborn.

These are the critical determinants of reproductive freedom and unfreedom in the New World Order, with its up-to-the-minute, technoscientifically mediated systems of flexible accumulation. Labour patterns, land use, capital accumulation and current kinds of class reformation might have more to do with the flow of breast milk than whether or not Nestlé has adopted policies of corporate responsibility in its Third World infant-formula markets. Artificial milk is a reproductive technology, without doubt, as is the human body itself, in all its historical/natural/technical complexity. But agribusiness seed technologies, which come with packages of labour and resource use, or marketing systems for national and international customers are at least as much reproductive technologies as are sonograph machines, Cesarean surgical operations or *in vitro* fertilization techniques. Those seeds and those marketing patterns are central techno-scientific actors, where humans and non-humans of many kinds are mutually enrolled in producing ways of life and death. It is high time that studies of reproductive technologies stop assuming that their central artifacts of interest are to be found only in the biomedical clinic. In several senses, computers in financial centres in Geneva, New York or Brasilia are reproductive technologies that have their bite in the breasts of marginalized women and the guts of their babies. It shows in the coffin-maker's invoices; the shelves of local grocery stores, where 'choice' is best studied; and, as we shall see, in (post)modern customs for establishing paternity among the poor.

Why do poor women stop breast feeding in the New World Order? How does technoscientifically mediated capital flow affect paternity-recognition rituals? Why can't 'rational choice' prevail in the *favelas* of the *Nordeste*, and perhaps also on the flatlands of the East Bay near San Francisco in California? Scheper-Hughes tells an arresting story about the corporeal economy of breast milk, diarrhea and family formation inside Brazil's economic miracle. With all its local themes and variations, the story travels globally all-too-well. It encapsulates one of the plot structures of postmodern narration – one left out of semiotic textbooks and psychoanalytical theory – in which gender, race, class and nation get up-to-the-minute remakes.

Loosely following Scheper-Hughes' map, let us explore the parameters of breast feeding. In the 1960s the US-sponsored Food for Peace programme introduced large amounts of industrially produced powdered milk into the Third World. A food inscribed with a better technoscientific pedigree and radiating more enlightened purposes would be hard to find. International aid-promoted, packaged baby milk programmes ended in the 1970s; but corporations like Nestlé moved in to develop the infant-formula market. Much of this market depends on very small purchases at any one time, not unlike the soft drink industry among the impoverished. Marketing infant formula to the poor is like marketing drugs – small, cheap packages are essential to hooking the customers and developing the mass market. Active organizing emerged against the aggressive, medically inflected marketing of artificial formula to women who could not afford the product over the long haul, nor count on conditions to prepare it hygienically. After a lot of denial and resistance, in response to an international boycott started in 1978, Nestlé finally adopted codes for ethical practice and modified its marketing and advertising patterns. But breast feeding continued to decline, and infant death continued to be modernized. 'Ethics' turns out to have precious little to do with 'choice' in vast areas of technoscience, including the yearning for reproductive freedom.

Four factors converge in this story. First, Scheper-Hughes found that the *culture* of breast feeding unraveled over a brief period – including both the ability of older women to teach younger women and also poor women's belief in the goodness of what comes from their own bodies, compared to what comes from 'modern' objects, like cans or hypodermic needles.[12] To emphasize that breast feeding is practice and culture, just as technoscience is practice and culture, is to stress that the body is simultaneously a historical, natural, technical, discursive and material entity. Breast milk is not nature to the culture of Nestlé's formula. Both fluids are natural-technical objects, embedded in matrices of practical culture and cultural practice. Women can lose, regain or improve the natural-technical knowledge necessary to breast feeding, just as young elephants can lose the ability to find water in long droughts when most of the older, knowledgeable animals are killed by poaching or by inexpert culling of herds. That comparison is not a naturalization of women, but an insistence on the shared natural-technical matter of living as intelligent mortal creatures on this planet. Within the kind of feminist technoscience studies that makes sense to me, breast-feeding practices, elephant cultural transmission and laboratory and factory knowledge and commodity production are ontologically and epistemologically similar. Historical ways of life and death are at stake in each of the natural-technical categories. The differences lie in the all-important specificities.

Second, and related to loss of knowledge about how or whether to breast feed, poor women cannot breast feed babies in the context of the jobs that they can get after the transition from semi-subsistence peasant to urban casual day labourer, including current forms of domestic service. The issue goes way beyond the Brazilian *favela* that Scheper-Hughes studied. Just as right-wing Californian politicians can and do agitate for withholding medical and educational benefits from the children of the migrant women who take care of these same politician-employers' offspring, modern female employers of other women can and do discourage practices that the wealthy reserve for themselves in the interest of health and family. Breast-milk storage equipment notwithstanding, babies have to be with mothers in order to breast feed consistently. On-the-job breast-feeding facilities, as well as other aspects of affordable and comprehensive childcare, remain pie-in-the-sky labour demands in most places of employment in the US. Discursively, such facilities are costly benefits, not natural rights. It is no wonder that poor women in and out of the 'Third World' have much less chance to 'choose' breast feeding, even if they continue, in spite of everything, to trust their own – disproportionately poisoned – bodies to give better nutrition than modern commodities can.[13]

Third, the shelves in the groceries that served the shantytown citizens were replete with every sort of scientifically formulated milk for infants. Literate or not, the mothers were well versed in all the varieties and their relative merits for babies of different ages and conditions. 'The array of "choices" was quite daunting, and the display of infant-formula powdered milk tins and boxes took up a full aisle of the local supermarket, more than for any other food product' (Scheper-Hughes, 1992: 319). Like the mandatory health warning on cigarette packages in the United States, which disproportionately fill the poorest areas of cities, all the infant milk containers carried required warnings about proper use of the product, consulting a physician and refrigeration. Consumer protection is such an illuminating practice in transnational capital's progressive regulatory regimes.

Fourth and last, let us turn to a scenario of family formation, to the kind of scene beloved in psychoanalytic contributions to feminist theory. I am particularly interested here in the material/semiotic rituals that create fathers and in the practices that relocate baby's milk from the breasts disdained by responsible, loving women to the packages – replete with corporate and state warnings – carried into the home by responsible, loving men. I am interested in the metonymy that marks the implantation of the name of the father in the *favela* and in what such substitutions do to the formation of the 'unconscious' in feminist technoscience studies. I believe this kind of unconscious underlies practices of yearning, oppositional consciousness and situated knowledges. The primal scene in the *favela* is established and signified by a gift of milk. Father's milk, not semen, is his means of confirming paternity and establishing the legitimacy of his child.

Scheper-Hughes tells that in the conditions of shantytown life, marriage becomes much more informal, consensual and, in my ironic terms, 'postmodern'. 'Shantytown households and families are "made up" through a creative form of bricolage in which we can think of a mother and her children as the stable core and husbands and fathers as detachable, circulating units. . . . A husband is a man who provides food for his woman and her children, regardless of whether he is living with them.' The symbolic transaction by which a father 'claims' his child and his woman is to bring the infant's first weeks' supply of Nestogeno, an especially valued Nestlé product in a lovely purple can. A woman who breast feeds is thought of as an abandoned woman, or a woman otherwise unprovided for or sexually disdained by a man. Ideally, the equation is, 'Papa: baby's "milk"' (Scheper-Hughes, 1992: 323–5). Through that particular and historical milk, meanings of paternity circulate. In this specific narration of metonymy and substitution, a powerful version of feminist desire is born. The desire is not for a supposed natural mother over and against a violating father, but for a new world order in which women, men and children can be linked in signifying chains that articulate the situated semiotic and material terms of reproductive freedom.

The missing babies of the *favela* are carried away in diarrhea, a 'sea of froth and brine. . . . "They die," said one woman going straight to the heart of the matter, "because their bodies turn to water"' (Scheper-Hughes, 1992: 303). Through the signifying flow of commodified milk – which links children and fathers, husbands and wives, First and Third Worlds, centres and margins, capital and bodies, milk and excrement, anthropologist and clerk of the records – we are recirculated back into the turbulent,

FEMINIST REVIEW NO 55, SPRING 1997

heterogeneous rivers of information that constitute the embryo, fetus and baby as a modern *sacrum* – or cyborg kinship entity – on the globalized planet earth. The diarrhea of angels mixes with the amniotic fluid of on-screen fetuses. We are accountable for this material and semiotic anasto-mosis in the body politic and the clinical body of the 'postmodern' human family. The longing to understand and change the fluid dynamics inherent in this kind of anastomosis is what I mean by yearning in feminist techno-science studies.

The signifying chains that make up these kinds of linkages are not, in any simple sense, about cause and effect. The multi-dimensional splices that bind together the New World Order, Inc. cannot be described in linear equations. But these higher-order linkages matter; they are not decorative flourishes. One task of feminist technoscience studies is to construct the analytical lan-guages – to design the speculums – for representing and intervening in our spliced, cyborg worlds. In the Bell Telephone ad, paternity was channelled from the phone through the mother-to-be's touching the sonographic image of the fetus on the video-monitor. In the *favela* of the *Nordeste*, paternity was channelled through the gift of scientifically formulated, commodified infant milk. The signifiers of choice for Bell Telephone and for Nestlé parody feminist reproductive freedom and knowledge projects and the dispersed, disseminated, differentiated, 'transnational' yearning that sustains them. In Kelly's cartoon, reproductive choice was interrogated in First Women's authorial touch on the computer keyboard. In Charlotte Rutherford's argu-ments about reproductive freedom for African-American women, the sta-tistics of inequality bore eloquent testimony to the reproduction of unfreedom. All of these accounts are aspects of the inquiry into reproduc-tive technology in the New World Order. As Wonder Woman put it in 1973, 'With my speculum, I am strong! I can fight!' The right speculum for the job makes visible the data structures that are our bodies.

> It was a dry wind
> And it swept across the desert
> And it curled into the circle of birth
> And the dead sand
> Falling on the children
> The Mothers and the Fathers
> And the Automatic Earth
> And don't cry, Baby, don't cry.

© 1986 Paul Simon/Paul Simon Music (BMI)

Notes

Donna Haraway is a professor in the History of Consciousness Board at the University of California at Santa Cruz, where she teaches feminist theory, science studies and women's studies. She is the author of *Crystals, Fabrics and Fields: Metaphors of Organicism in Twentieth-Century Developmental Biology* (1976, New Haven: Yale University Press), *Primate Visions: Gender, Race, and Nature in the World of Modern Science* (1989, New York and London: Routledge; 1992, London: Verso), *Simians, Cyborgs, and Women: The Reinvention of Nature* (1991, London: Free Association Books; 1991, New York: Routledge), and a new book, *Modest_Witness@Second_Millennium.FemaleMan©_Meets_OncoMouse*™ (1996, New York and London: Routledge).

I would like especially to thank Adele Clarke, Valerie Hartouni, Stefan Helmreich, Lynn Randolph, and the Bay Area Technology and Culture Group for comments on 'The Virtual Speculum'.

1 A revised version of this essay is forthcoming in Donna Haraway, *Modest_Witness@Second_Millennium.FemaleMan©_Meets_OncoMouse*™ (1996, New York and London: Routledge).

2 Teresa de Lauretis gave me a copy of an early thirteenth-century 'virtual speculum' called *The Creation of Eve*, from the Creation Dome in the entrance hall in the Basilica di S. Marco in Venice. In this flat, iconic, narrative painting, God is bending over the sleeping Adam in the Garden of Eden and extracting from his side the rib that will be formed into the first man's wife and companion. This is not the creation scene that has inspired the iconographers of technoscientific advertising, conference brochures and magazine-cover design. For these twentieth-century graphic artists, on the other hand, the touch between God and Adam depicted by Michelangelo has incited orgies of visual quotation. See magazine covers for *Omni* April 1983, *Time* 8 November 1993, and *Discover* August 1992. For fans of Escher in the Artificial Life community, studied ethnographically by Stefan Helmreich (1995), the poster image for the second ALife conference features a visual quotation from *The Creation of Adam* in the cyberspace mode. This creation scene takes place at night, with a quarter moon shining through a window that is also a screen onto the starry universe. Describing the image, Helmreich (personal communication, 18 May 1995) writes, 'The notion that Man replaces God and renders Woman irrelevant in the new creations of Artificial Life is vividly illustrated . . . in a poster for the second workshop on Artificial Life, in which a white male programmer touches his finger to a keyboard to meet the waiting fingers of a skeletal circuit-based artificial creature (itself somewhat masculine).' The programmer himself is a kind of merman figure; the head and torso is of a human male, but the bottom half is a video display terminal, whose nether end hooks into the eye of the circuit-skeletal figure. The Escheresque circular composition, full of arrows and fractal recursive shapes connoting self organization, is a kind of uroborus, eating its own electronic tail in an orgy of self creation. The men who got the conference together called themselves the 'self-organizing committee'. The conference was sponsored by the Center for Non-Linear Studies at the Los Alamos National Laboratory in 1990.

3 Gross and Levitt (1994) outrageously caricature the feminist science studies insistence on the contingency of 'reality' and the constructedness of science. It is important that my account of reality as an effect of an interaction, as opposed to a treasure awaiting discovery, not be misunderstood. 'Reality' is certainly not 'made up' in scientific practice; but it is collectively, materially and semiotically constructed – that is, put together, made to cohere, worked up for and by us in some ways and not others. This is not a relativist position, if by relativism one means that the facts and models, including mathematical models, of natural scientific accounts of the world are merely matters of desire, opinion, specu-lation, fantasy, or any other such 'mental' faculty. Science is a practice, an inter-action inside and with worlds. Science is not a doctrine or a set of observer-independent, but still empirically grounded (how?) statements about some ontologically separate nature-not-culture. Minimally, an observing inter-action requires historically located human beings; particular apparatuses, which might include devices like the hominid visual-brain system and the instruments of perspective drawing; and a heterogeneous world, in which people and instru-ments are immersed and which is always pre-structured within material-semi-otic fields. 'Observers' are not just people, much less disembodied minds; observers are also non-human entities, sometimes called inscription devices, to which people have materially delegated observation, often precisely to make it 'impersonal'. (As we will see below, statistics can be one of those instruments for making reality impersonal.) 'Impersonal' does not mean 'observer-indepen-dent'. Reality is not a 'subjective' construction, but a congealing of ways of inter-acting that makes the opposition of subjective and objective grossly misleading. These ways of interacting require the dense array of bodies, artifacts, minds, col-lectives, etc. that make up any rich world. The opposition of 'knowing minds', on one hand, and 'material reality' awaiting description, on the other hand, is a silly set-up. Reality is eminently material and solid; but the effects sedimented out of the technologies of observation/representation are radically contingent in the sense that other semiotic-material-technical processes of observation would (and do) produce quite different lived worlds, including cognitively lived worlds, not just different statements about worlds as observer-independent arrays of objects. I think that is a richer, more adequate, less ideological account than Gross and Levitt's insistence that science is reality driven (1994: 234). Obviously, neither I nor any other science studies person, feminist or otherwise, whom I have ever met or read, mean the 'laws of physics' get suspended if one enters a 'different' culture. That is a laughable notion of both physical laws and cultural, historical difference. It is the position that Gross and Levitt, in deliberate bad faith or else astonishingly deficient reading, ascribe to me and other feminist science studies writers. My argument tries to avoid the silly oppositions of rela-tivism and realism. Rather, I am interested in how an observation-situation pro-duces quite 'objective' worlds, worlds not subject to 'subjective' preference or mere opinion, but worlds that must be lived in consequence in some ways and

not others. For a theory of 'agential realism', to which my arguments about 'situated knowledges' are closely related, see Barad (1995).

4 This title is in honor of Clarke and Fujimura (1992).

5 Boston Women's Health Book Collective (1976); *Nuestros Cuerpos, Nuestras Vidas* (1979). The Boston Women's Health Book Collective began putting out *Our Bodies, Ourselves* in newsprint form in the 1970s as an integral part of activist health struggles. For a bibliography of the early women's health movement and feminist science and medicine studies from the 1970s, see Hubbard, Henifin, and Fried (1982). Despite its extensive concern with instruments and tools, practices in and out of the laboratory, and science-in-the-making, the kind of activist-based material in Hubbard *et al.*'s bibliography is systematically excluded from professional, academic histories of science and technology studies. See, for example, Knorr-Cetina and Mulkay (1983).

6 See, for example, Committee for Abortion Rights and against Sterilization Abuse (1979); Coalition for the Reproductive Rights of Workers (1980); Black Women's Community Development Foundation (1975); Davis (1981); Smith (1982); White (1990). This literature reflects the dominance of the black–white racial polarity of US society and understates the presence and priorities of other racial-ethnic women in women's health and reproductive politics of that period. See Moraga and Anzaldúa (1981).

7 I am in permanent debt to Nancy Hartsock's (1983) pioneering formulation of non-essentialist feminist standpoint theory. Standpoint theories are not private reservations for different species of human beings, innate knowledge available only to victims, or special pleading. Within feminist theory in Hartsock's lineage, standpoints are cognitive-emotional-political achievements, crafted out of located social-historical-bodily experience – itself always constituted through fraught, non-innocent, material, collective practices – that could make less deluded knowledge for all of us more likely. My arguments in 'Virtual Speculum' also draw from Harding (1992) on strong objectivity as a mode of extended critical examination of knowledge-producing apparatuses and agents; Collins (1991) on the internally heterogeneous and insider/outsider locations that have nurtured Black feminist thought; Star (1991) on viewing standards from the point of view of those who do not fit them but must live within them; Butler (1992) on contingent foundations as achievements and agency as practice rather than attribute; Haraway (1988) on situated knowledges in scientific epistemology and the refusal of the ideological choice between realism and relativism; hooks (1990) on yearning – rooted in the historical experience of oppression and inequality, but unimpressed by stances of victimhood – that can bind knowledge and action across difference; Sandoval (forthcoming) on the potential of learning and teaching oppositional consciousness across multiple and intersecting differentiations of race, gender, nationality, sexuality and class; Bhavnani (1993) on feminist objectivity within a polyglot world; and Tsing (1993) on multiple centres and margins and on the stunning complexity and specificity of local–global cross talk and circulations of power and knowledge. That Hartsock, Harding, Hill-Collins, Star, Bhavnani, Tsing, Haraway, Sandoval, hooks and Butler are not supposed to agree about postmodernism, standpoints, science studies or feminist theory is neither my problem or theirs. The problem is the needless yet common cost of taxonimizing everyone's positions without regard to the contexts of their development, or of refusing rereading and overlayering in order to make new patterns from previous disputes. I am recontextualizing all of this writing to make a case for how thinking about reproductive freedom should make its practitioners reconfigure how to do technoscience studies *in general*. Theory and practice develop precisely through such recontextualization. For learning to read the always topographically complex history of feminist theory (and theory projects broadly), see King (1994).

8 Adele Clarke (personal communication, 16 May 1995) reminded me of the history of recent feminist efforts to build reproductive policy from the standpoints of the most vulnerable, e.g., the explicit programme of the Reproductive Rights National Network in the 1970s and 1980s. Clarke recounted the example of the passage of sterilization regulations in California, which applied to all sterilizations, not just those funded by Medicaid. Developed by the Committee for Abortion Rights and against Sterilization Abuse (CARASA), national sterilization regulations applied only to Medicaid recipients. Shepherded by the Committee to Defend Reproductive Rights, the California regulations – the only ones to pass on a state level – were the fruit of difficult coalition-building between middle-class, mostly white women from the National Organization for Women, who were more affected by inaccessible sterilization, and working-class and non-white women's groups, who were more impacted by abusive sterilization. In the 1990s, the ordinary situation of multiple and heterogeneous vulnerabilities and capabilities, which imply conflicting policy needs, demands urgent feminist attention in local and global dimensions. The International Reproductive Rights Research Action Group (IRRRAG) is a collaborative, multicountry research project on the meanings of reproductive rights to women in diverse cultural settings. See Petchesky and Weiner (1990). Written by an international group of feminist activists and scholars, the papers in Ginsberg and Rapp (1995) put reproduction at the centre of social theory in general and, through detailed and culturally alert analyses, show how pregnancy, parenting, birth control, population policies, demography and the new reproductive technologies shape and are shaped by differently situated women. Non-reductive feminist reproductive discourse and policy can flourish in this context. For example, Barroso and Corrêa (1995: 292–306) show how the difficult interactions of feminists and researchers around the introduction of Norplant into Brazil resulted ultimately in raised public consciousness, attention to informed consent in Norms of Research on Health approved by the Ministry of Health, and effective local ethics committees. Non-feminist approaches to reproductive technologies still abound everywhere. At the 1994 American Fertility Society's 50th Anniversary Meetings in San Antonio, Texas, a Norplant ad poster prominently featured the words, 'Compliance-free contraceptive'. Thanks to Charis Cussins for a photograph of the poster.

9 For the story of public health statistics intrinsic to freedom projects in the twentieth-century United States, see Elizabeth Fee and Nancy Krieger, 'What's Class Got to Do with Health? A Critique of Biomedical Individualism,' paper presented to the Meeting of the Society for Social Studies of Science, New

Orleans, 12–16 October, 1994. For a view of a feminist economics think-tank, see the publications of the Washington, D.C., Institute for Women's Policy Research, co-founded by Heidi Hartman, winner of a 1994 MacArthur Fellowship for her work, e.g., Spalter-Roth *et al.* (1995).

10 In order, figures and quotes are taken from the following pages in Rutherford: 257n8, 258n11, 259n12, 260, 260n15, 264n32, 265n38, 266n45, 267, 268, 268n56, 268n61, 273–4, 280, 280n128.

11 Stefan Helmreich pointed out to me a particularly egregious racial-sexual rendering of r and K selection arguments, with people of African descent having more extramarital affairs, Black men having longer penises, Black women having shorter menstrual cycles, and a host of other racist-sexist pseudo-facts leading to the conclusion of different evolutionary strategies among (leaving aside the problem of the biological reality of the categories) White, Black and Oriental populations (Rushton and Bogaert, 1987).

12 'In Brazil the decline in breast-feeding has been precipitous; between 1940 and 1975 the percentage of babies breast-fed *for any length of time* fell from 96% to less than 40%. . . . Since that time it has decreased even further' (Scheper-Hughes, 1992: 317). Breast feeding has also declined in the US. In 1993, only 50 percent of all new mothers initiated breast feeding while in the hospital, and only 19 percent persisted after six months. In the United States, breast feeding is also deeply differentiated by class and race, with the most privileged groups 'choosing' breast feeding the most often, and their less-well-off sisters 'choosing' artificial formula. For example, 70 percent of college-educated mothers breast fed their infants at birth, compared to 43 percent of those with a high-school education and 32 percent of those with an elementary-school education; 23 percent of Black mothers breast fed their babies at birth, compared to 59 percent of White mothers (Blum, 1993: 299). Through its Women, Infants, and Children Program (WIC), the US government purchases about $1.7 billion of formula per year for use by poor mothers, covering about 40 percent of all US babies (Baker, 1995: 25). Advertising by formula companies remains a big issue, and it works in conjunction with the absence of childcare and maternal support policies that would make breast feeding feasible for economically disadvantaged people.

13 Lest we lose site of enterpreneurial biotechnology in this essay, genetic engineering is on the way to duplicating human breast milk. The product could be sold to affluent mothers (or bought by public health agencies or health maintenance organizations), whose own milk might not be quite the thing or whose children might not thrive on current artificial milk. Dutch research with cows involves bovine transgenics with milk-specific human genes, so that the animals' secretion mimics the human fluid. See Crouch (1995). I am not opposed to this research as a violation of intimate female experience and cultural categories of nature; but, like Crouch, I am highly skeptical that this research would do as much to improve babies' and mothers' health as similar amounts of R&D money spent on maternal support policies that increased ordinary breast feeding or on environmental policies that reduced the toxin burden in women's bodies all over the world.

References

ALLEN, Patricia (1994) *The Human Face of Sustainable Agriculture: Adding People to the Environmental Agenda*, Center for Agroecology and Sustainable Food Systems, University of California at Santa Cruz. Sustainability in the Balance Series (Issue Paper No. 4).

AUERBACH, Erich (1953) *Mimesis: The Representation of Reality in Western Literature* Princeton: Princeton University Press.

BAKER, Linda (1995) 'Message in a bottle' *In These Times* Vol. 19, No. 20: 24–6.

BARAD, Karen (1995) 'Meeting the universe halfway: ambiguities, discontinuities, quantum subjects, and multiple positionings in feminism and physics' in **Nelson** and **Nelson,** editors *Feminism, Science, and the Philosophy of Science: A Dialogue.* Norwell, MA: Kluwer Press.

BARROSO, Carmen and CORRÊA, Sônia (1995) 'Public servants, professionals, and feminists: the politics of contraceptive research in Brazil' in **Ginsberg** and **Rapp** (1995).

BHAVNANI, Kum-Kum (1993) 'Tracing the contours: feminist research and feminist objectivity' *Women's Studies International Forum* Vol. 16, No. 2: 95–104.

BLACK WOMEN'S COMMUNITY DEVELOPMENT FOUNDATION (BWCDF) (1975) *Mental and Physical Health Problems of Black Women* Washington, DC: BWCDF.

BLEECKER, Julian (1995) 'Urban crisis: past, present, and virtual' *Socialist Review* Vol. 25, No. 1 (Winter).

BLUM, Linda M. (1993) 'Mothers, babies, and breastfeeding in late capitalist America: the shifting contexts of feminist theory' *Feminist Studies* Vol. 19, No. 2: 291–311.

BOSTON WOMEN'S HEALTH BOOK COLLECTIVE (BWHBC) (1976) *Our Bodies, Ourselves: A Book by and for Women* 2nd edn New York: Simon & Schuster.

BOSTON WOMEN'S HEALTH BOOK COLLECTIVE (BWHBC) (1979) *Nuestros Cuerpos, Nuestras Vidas* Somerville, MA: BWHBC, Inc.

BRAIDOTTI, Rosi (1994) *Nomadic Subjects: Embodiment and Subjectivity in Contemporary Feminist Theory* New York: Columbia University Press.

BUTLER, Judith (1992) 'Contingent foundations: feminism and the question of postmodernism' in **Butler** and **Scott,** editors *Feminists Theorize the Political* New York: Routledge.

CASPER, Monica (1995a) 'Fetal cyborgs and technomoms on the reproductive frontier: which way to the carnival?' in **Gray, Figueroa-Sarriera** and **Mentor** (1995).

CASPER, Monica (1995b) 'The making of the unborn patient: medical work and the politics of reproduction in experimental fetal surgery, 1963–1993'. Ph.D. diss., Graduate Program in Sociology, University of California at San Francisco.

CLARK, Timothy J. (1985) *The Painting of Modern Life: Paris in the Art of Manet and his Followers* New York: Knopf.

CLARKE, Adele and FUJIMURA, Joan (eds) (1992) *The Right Tools for the Job: At Work in Twentieth-Century Life Sciences* Princeton: Princeton University Press.

CLARKE, Adele and Teresa MONTINI (1993) 'The many faces of RU486: tales of situated knowledges and technological contestations' *Science, Technology, and Human Values* Vol. 18, No. 1: 42–78.

COALITION FOR THE REPRODUCTIVE RIGHTS OF WORKERS (CRROW) (1980) *Reproductive Hazards in the Workplace: A Resource Guide* Washington, DC: CRROW.

COLLINS, Patricia Hill (1991) *Black Feminist Thought: Knowledge, Consciousness, and the Politics of Empowerment* New York: Routledge.

COMMITTEE FOR ABORTION RIGHTS AND AGAINST STERILIZATION ABUSE (CARASA) (1979) *Women under Attack: Abortion, Sterilization Abuse, and Reproductive Freedom* New York: CARASA.

CROUCH, Martha L. (1995) 'Like mother used to make?' *The Women's Review of Books* Vol. XII, No. 5: 31–2.

CUSSINS, Charis (1996) 'Ontological choreography: agency through objectification in infertility clinics' *Social Studies of Science* Vol. 26, No. 3.

DALY, Martin and WILSON, Margo (1978) *Sex, Evolution, and Behavior: Adaptations for Reproduction* North Scituate, MA: Duxbury Press.

DAVIS, Angela (1981) *Women, Race and Class* New York: Random House.

DOWNEY, Gary and DUMIT, Joseph (eds) (forthcoming) *Cyborgs and Citadels: Anthropological Interventions on the Borderlands of Technoscience* Seattle: University of Washington Press.

DUDEN, Barbara (1993) *Disembodying Women: Perspectives on Pregnancy and the Unborn* Cambridge: Harvard University Press.

EDGAR, Joanne (1972) 'Wonder woman revisited' *Ms.* Vol. 1, No. 1: 52–5.

EHRENREICH, Barbara and ENGLISH, Deirdre (1973) *Complaints and Disorders: The Sexual Politics of Sickness* Old Westbury, NY: The Feminist Press.

ESCOBAR, Arturo (1994) 'Welcome to cyberia: notes on the anthropology of cyberculture' *Current Anthropology* Vol. 35, No. 3: 211–31.

FAIRCHILD, Halford (1991) 'Scientific racism: the cloak of objectivity' *Journal of Social Issues* Vol. 47, No. 3: 101–16.

FEE, Elizabeth and KRIEGER, Nancy (1994) 'What's class got to do with health? A critique of biomedical individualism', paper read at Meeting of the Society for Social Studies of Science, 12–16 October, at New Orleans.

FLOWER, Michael (n.d.) 'Technoscientific liberty', unpublished manuscript, University Honors Program, Portland State University.

FOUCAULT, Michel (1978) *The History of Sexuality*, translated by Robert Hurley, Vol. 1: *An Introduction* New York: Pantheon.

FRANKLIN, Sarah (1993a) 'Making representations: the parliamentary debate on the human fertilisation and embryology act' in **Edwards, Franklin, Hirsch, Price** and **Strathern**, editors *Technologies of Procreation: Kinship in the Age of Assisted Conception* Manchester: Manchester University Press.

FRANKLIN, Sarah (1993b) 'Life itself', paper delivered at Centre for Cultural Values, Lancaster University, 9 June.

GASPERINI, Jim (1994) 'The miracle of good multimedia' *Wired* (February): 198.

GINSBERG, Faye and RAPP, Rayna (1991) 'The politics of reproduction' *Annual Reviews in Anthropology* Vol. 20: 311–43.

GINSBERG, Faye and RAPP, Rayna (eds) (1995) *Conceiving the New World Order: The Global Politics of Reproduction* Los Angeles: University of California Press.

GINSBERG, Faye D. and TSING, Anna L. (eds) (1990) *Uncertain Terms: Negotiating Gender in American Culture* Boston: Beacon Press.

GRAY, Chris, FIGUEROA-SARRIERA, Heidi and MENTOR, Steven (eds) (1995) *The Cyborg Handbook* New York: Routledge.

GROSS, Paul R. and LEVITT, Norman (1994) *Higher Superstition: The Academic Left and Its Quarrels with Science* Baltimore: Johns Hopkins University Press.

HAMILTON, Joan O'C. (1994) 'Biotech: an industry crowded with players faces an ugly reckoning' *Business Week* (26 September): 84–90.

HAMPTON, Henry (1986–87) *Eyes on the prize: America's civil rights years, 1954–65* Alexandria, VA/Boston, MA: Blackside, Inc., and CPB for WGBH Boston. Television series.

HARAWAY, Donna J. (1988) 'Situated knowledges: the science question in feminism as a site of discourse on the privilege of partial perspective' *Feminist Studies* Vol. 14, No. 3: 575–99.

HARAWAY, Donna J. (1994) 'Never modern, never been, never ever: some thoughts about never-never land in science studies', paper read at Meeting of the Society for Social Studies of Science, 12–16 October, at New Orleans.

HARDING, Susan (1990) 'If I die before I wake' in **Ginsberg** and **Tsing** (1990).

HARDING, Sandra (1992) *Whose Science? Whose Knowledge? Thinking from Women's Lives* Ithaca: Cornell University Press.

HARTOUNI, Valerie (1991) 'Containing women: reproductive discourse in the 1980s' in **Penley** and **Ross**, editors *Technoculture* Minneapolis: University of Minnesota Press.

HARTOUNI, Valerie (1992) 'Fetal exposures: abortion politics and the optics of allusion' *Camera Obscura: A Journal of Feminism and Film Theory* Vol. 29: 130–49.

HARTOUNI, Valerie (1996) *Making Life Make Sense: New Technologies and the Discourses of Reproduction* Minneapolis: University of Minnesota Press.

HARTSOCK, Nancy (1983) 'The feminist standpoint: developing the ground for a specifically feminist historical materialism' in **Harding** and **Hintikka**, editors *Discovering Reality: Feminist Perspectives on Epistemology, Methodology, and Philosophy of Science* Dordrecht/Boston: Reidel.

HARVEY, David (1989) *The Condition of Postmodernity: An Enquiry into the Origins of Cultural Change* Oxford: Basil Blackwell.

HAYS, Denys (1967) *The Age of the Renaissance* New York: McGraw-Hill.

HELMREICH, Stefan (1995) 'Anthropology inside and outside the looking-glass worlds of artificial life', Ph.D. diss., Department of Anthropology, Stanford University.

hooks, bell (1990) *Yearning* Boston: Southend Press.

HUBBARD, Ruth, HENIFIN, Mary Sue and FRIED, Barbara (eds) (1982) *Biological Woman – The Convenient Myth: A Collection of Feminist Essays and a Comprehensive Bibliography* Cambridge: Schenkman.

JANSEN, H. W. and JANSEN, Dora Jane (1963) *History of Art* Englewood Cliffs/New York: Prentice Hall and Harry N. Abrams.

KING, Katie (1994) *Theory in Its Feminist Travels: Conversations in U.S. Women's Movements* Bloomington: Indiana University Press.

KNORR-CETINA, Karin and MULKAY, Michael (eds) (1983) *Science Observed: Perspectives on the Social Study of Science* Beverly Hills: Sage Publications.

LATOUR, Bruno (1993) *We Have Never Been Modern*, translated by Porter Cambridge: Harvard University Press.

LORDE, Audre (1984) 'The master's tools will never dismantle the master's house' in Lorde, *Sister Outsider: Essays and Speeches* Trumansburg, NY: Crossing Press.

MACARTHUR, R. H. (1962) 'Some generalized theorems of natural selection' *Proceedings of the National Academy of Sciences* Vol. 48: 1893–7.

MORAGA, Cherríe and ANZALDÚA, Gloria (eds) (1981) *This Bridge Called My Back: Writings by Radical Women of Color* Watertown, MA: Persephone Press.

NATIONS, Marilyn K. and REBHUN, L. A. (1988) 'Angels with wet wings won't fly: maternal sentiment in Brazil and the image of neglect' *Culture, Medicine and Psychiatry* Vol. 12: 141–200.

NEAD, Lynda (1992) *The Female Nude: Art, Obscenity and Sexuality* New York: Routledge.

NILSSON, Lennart (1977) *A Child Is Born* New York: Dell.

NILSSON, Lennart (1987) *The Body Victorious: The Illustrated Story of our Immune System and Other Defenses of the Human Body* New York: Delacourt.

NILSSON, Lennart and HAMBERGER, Lars (1994) *A Child Is Born* Philips. CD-I.

PETCHESKY, Rosalind Pollock (1987) 'Fetal images: the power of visual culture in the politics of reproduction' *Feminist Studies* Vol. 13, No. 2: 263–92.

PETCHESKY, Rosalind Pollack and WEINER, Jennifer (1990) *Global Feminist Perspectives on Reproductive Rights and Reproductive Health* New York: Hunter College/Reproductive Rights Education Project.

PICKERING, Andrew (ed.) (1992) *Science as Practice and Culture* Chicago: University of Chicago Press.

PORTER, Theodore M. (1994) 'Objectivity as standardization: the rhetoric of impersonality in measurement, statistics, and cost-benefit analysis' in McGill, editor *Rethinking Objectivity* Durham: Duke University Press.

PORTER, Theodore M. (1995) *Trust in Numbers: The Pursuit of Objectivity in Science and Public Life* Princeton: Princeton University Press.

RANDOLPH, Lynn (1993) 'The Ilusas (deluded women): representations of women who are out of bounds', paper delivered at The Bunting Institute, 30 November.

RAPP, Rayna (1994) 'Refusing prenatal diagnostic technology: the uneven meanings of bioscience in a multicultural world', paper read at Society for Social Studies of Science, 12–16 October, at New Orleans.

RAPP, Rayna (forthcoming) 'Real time fetus: the role of the sonogram in the age of monitored reproduction' in Downey and Dumit, editors.

RUSHTON, J. Philippe and BOGAERT, Anthony F. (1987) 'Race differences in sexual behavior: testing an evolutionary hypothesis' *Journal of Research in Personality* Vol. 21: 529–51.

RUTHERFORD, Charlotte (1992) 'Reproductive freedoms and African American women' *Yale Journal of Law and Feminism* Vol. 4, No. 2: 255–90.

SANDOVAL, Chéla (forthcoming) *Oppositional Consciousness in the Postmodern World* Minneapolis: University of Minnesota Press.

SCHEPER-HUGHES, Nancy (1992) *Death without Weeping: The Violence of Everyday Life in Brazil* Berkeley/Los Angeles: University of California Press.

SIMON, Paul (1986) 'The boy in the bubble' Warner Brothers Records, Inc. Song, from the album *Graceland*.

SMITH, Beverly (1982) 'Black women's health: notes for a course' in **Hubbard, Henifin** and **Fried**, editors.

SPALTER-ROTH, Roberta, BURR, Beverly, HARTMAN, Heidi and SHAW, Lois (1995) *Welfare That Works: The Working Life of AFDC Recipients* Washington, DC: Institute for Women's Policy Research.

STABEL, Ingse (1992) 'Den norske politiske debatten om bioteknologi' *Nytt om Kvinneforskning* Vol. 3: 43–8.

STABILE, Carol A. (1992) 'Shooting the mother: fetal photography and the politics of disappearance' *Camera Obscura: A Journal of Feminism and Film Theory* Vol. 28: 178–205.

STAR, Susan Leigh (1991) 'Power, technology and the phenomenology of conventions: on being allergic to onions' in **Law**, editor *A Sociology of Monsters: Power, Technology and the Modern World* Oxford: Basil Blackwell.

TREICHLER, Paula and CARTWRIGHT, Lisa (1992) 'Imaging technologies, inscribing science' *Camera Obscura: A Journal of Feminism and Film Theory* Nos 28 and 29.

TSING, Anna Lowenhaupt (1993) *In the Realm of the Diamond Queen: Marginality in an Out-of-the-Way Place* Princeton: Princeton University Press.

WHITE, Evelyn (ed.) (1990) *The Black Women's Health Book* Seattle: Seal Press.

Bridging the Gap:

Feminism, Fashion and Consumption

Angela McRobbie

FEMINIST REVIEW NO 55, SPRING 1997, pp. 73–89

Abstract

The article confronts two issues, first the question of women and consumption and second the fashion industry as a feminized sector. In the first instance the argument is that recent scholarship on consumption has been weakened by an inattention to questions of exclusion from consumption and the production of consumption. Income differentials as well as questions of poverty have dropped off the agenda in this debate. Attention instead has been paid to the meaning systems which come into play around items of consumption. This has led to a sense of political complacency as though consumption is not a problem. For the many thousands of women bringing up children at or below the poverty line it clearly is. The second part of the article takes the fashion industry as an example of a field where perspectives on both production and consumption are rarely brought together. This produces a sense of political hopelessness in relation to improving its employment practices, especially for very low paid women workers. The argument here is that greater integration and debate across the production and consumption divide could conceivably result in policies which would make this sector whose employees on a global basis are predominantly female, a better place of work.

Keywords

gender; consumption; modernity; fashion

The Social Relations of Consumption

This piece is written partly out of a sense of frustration that so much recent writing on women and consumption has been flawed by an inattention to the processes of exclusion which structure and limit access to consumption. These of course are largely to do with disposable income. But there are additional absences in this work which have to do with specificities and particularities in regard to consumption, that is with how different groups of women, from different class and ethnic backgrounds, actually experience this thing called consumption. Indeed there often seems to be a wilful avoidance of questions of poverty and hardship. Nor is there any emphasis on those who work at producing consumption. Both of these omissions contribute to a sense that 'we' can indeed all consume and that this process gives rise in our minds to no awkward questions about how much the shop assistant is being paid, or how, having purchased the weekly shopping, we will get through to the end of the month. Consumer culture is instead an arena of female participation and enjoyment. This runs the risk of inducing a sense of political complacency.

When feminist writers and cultural historians attempt to re-investigate the neglected field of consumption by showing how women were produced as the ideal subjects of consumption in early twentieth century America, or with the new role they were given following the growth of advertising and marketing in the inter-war years, or with how women flocked to the department stores, my own reaction is to require some qualifications in this respect. They did not flock equally to consume. Nor was the invitation to consume extended to all women independent of means and status. On both sides of the Atlantic the imagined female consumer was invariably white and almost always middle class. And as we know from the direct experience of being treated with condescension or dismissal in upmarket department stores, shopping may be nominally open to all but this does not stop department stores from screening out 'unwanted customers'.[1] The status of the shop assistant is indicative in this respect. She is typically low-paid but is trained in accent and demeanour, with her job depending on her successful demonstration of these skills, to reflect the high-class quality of the goods. This practice dates back to the early days of the department store when wealthy customers complained of being put off the products by the unhealthy, poor-looking shop girls who were serving them.

For many, if not most, women throughout the periods described by authors such as Pumphrey (1987), Felski (1995), Nava (1996), Bowlby (1985) and Reekie (1995), i.e. from the mid-nineteenth century through the early years of this century, consumption has been an aggravated activity. It has most certainly been linked with the necessity of both paid work and also with unpaid work in the home. If women consumed fabrics, for example, it was to take home and make clothes for themselves and their children, unless of course they could pay other women to do this for them. So the act of consumption was merely the precursor for further domestic labour. While some of the above writers (e.g. Pumphrey and Reekie *en passant*) note the uneveness of women's ability to participate in consumption, the structures which produce and reproduce these divisions and the consequences these have for relations of power and powerlessness tend to be marginalized. Consumption is extrapolated from the broader sociological context in which purchasing is only one small part of a whole chain of productive activity.

As the academic interest in this field gains ground through the 1980s it is also surprising that instead of re-conceptualizing the traditional division between production and consumption to take into account the multiple levels of social and cultural as well as economic practices which traverse this divide, there is instead, in academic feminism over the last fifteen years, almost imperceptibly, a new division of labour which has emerged. Such a division suggests quite major political differences within feminism, though there is no space here to explore the fine nuances of disagreement and emphasis. Those who engage with issues of consumption (e.g. fashion), but from the viewpoint of production, could be described as 'materialist feminists', while those who are associated with the politics of meaning and with the world of texts and representations could be described as 'cultural feminists'.[2] In the former group figures including Rowbotham and Mitter (1994), Tate (1994) Phizacklea (1990) and others approach the world of goods from the viewpoint of the highly exploitative conditions under which these goods, usually items of fashion or clothing, have been produced by Third World women and children, often in sweat-shop conditions, or else by very poor First World women employed as homeworkers or in the small workshop units of North London and the West Midlands. Meanwhile feminists working in cultural and literary studies often tend to discount or overlook the material context of the production of consumption as indicative of a crudely economistic and reductionist approach, untuned to the level and meaning of female popular desires for consumer goods. In fact it is the concept of desire and with it pleasure which partly fuels this approach. Its worth briefly rehearsing that trajectory, as it is aspects of this that I now want to challenge.

The original argument was that the academic left including feminists too often felt the need to disavow their own participation in some of the pleasures of the consumer culture for the reason that these were the very epitome of capitalism and also one of the sources of women's oppression. This produced a culture of puritanism giving rise only to guilty pleasures. The study of popular culture in its most expanded sense allowed feminists to revise this traditional stance. The fact that many of these forms were also enjoyed by ordinary women allowed us to at least re-interrogate this terrain rather than to merely understand it as a site of 'false consciousness'. In addition through the 1980s the growth of a new kind of left and feminist cultural politics which involved exploring how more popular broad-based alliances could be forged made it possible to acknowledge the enjoyment people got from consumption (Hall, 1989; Mort, 1989, 1996). The issue here was of broadening out the political constituency to which the left could legitimately speak by including for example the newly affluent upper working and lower middle classes, i.e. the 'Daily Mail' terrain of support for Thatcherism. What seemed to happen, however, is that this momentum, combined as it was with speaking to other social identities and movements, resulted in the bottom end (whatever that might mean in economic terms) of the social hierarchy being dropped from the political and intellectual agenda. This raises the question of the terms and limits of popular left and feminist politics. Is it possible to address the very poor and the pretty affluent in the same political language? At any rate the interest in the practices of consumption was only rarely put to the test in the field of empirical investigation. Instead it was used to flag the conceptual autonomy of consumption away from the more problematic field of production. In effect it was about symbolic complexity, i.e. with all the unexpected things people do with items of consumption (Fiske, 1989). My argument now is that the emphasis has swung too far in this direction with little attempt being made to ask whether it is 'as much fun on the other side of the counter'.[3]

This writing suggests the far distance between contemporary consumer culture and the world of long hours, unrewarding work, drudgery and brutal exploitation. Celia Lury writes, for example, in the introduction to her recent volume that there is a 'relative independence of practices of consumption from those of production', this giving, she continues 'growing power and authority . . . to (at least some) consumers' (Lury, 1996: 4). Clearly this independence is a matter of where you look and where you stand in the labour market. In my own case the reality of homeworking was literally on my front doorstep. Neighbours on both sides of my last home in North London were up all night sewing, the lights were on and the gentle whirring of the sewing machines could be heard through the walls on either side. One was a Greek Cypriot woman whose 'bags' would be delivered early one morning and collected in exchange for finished work the next. On the other side of the wall an Asian grandmother also worked through the night and would then child-mind during the day having deposited her finished goods with her sons for delivery to the various street-markets of North and East London.

While there might be a case to argue that if the materialist feminists like Annie Phizacklea fail to look at what happens to the clothes once they leave the shops and enter the field of symbolic value then it is unfair to accuse the cultural feminists of ignoring questions of production and manufacture. The answer to this has got to be that while ideally both sides might be brought into dialogue with each other, there are more glaring political problems in the cultural feminists' avoidance of all questions of pain and suffering. This means that the whole basis of feminist scholarship, founded as it is upon interrogating issues of gender inequality and subordination, is somewhat jeopardized. Lury, for example, mentions poverty in the opening pages of her book and only returns to it once, fleetingly. 'Deprivation in contemporary Britain is widespread . . . it extends throughout the bottom half of society, becoming particularly acute in the bottom 30–40 per cent' (Lury, 1996: 5). These are hardly insignificant figures for any discussion of consumer culture, especially if we are concerned with how relations of inequality and of power and powerlessness are reproduced in society. Lury's 'bottom 30–40 per cent' would also doubtless include Phiza-cklea's Asian women homeworkers. Indeed if we take into account the feminization of poverty, the 'top half' of society with which Lury is primarily concerned becomes top heavy with men, and with white, wealthy middle England married couples. In effect she is talking about the privileged social classes.

The emphasis in the new consumerist studies is on what women and girls do with consumer goods and with how commodities give rise to meaning-making processes which are frequently at odds with the intended meaning or usage. Thus the 'world of goods' offers certain types of 'freedom' or even 'authority' to women as consumers with these taking on overtones of sexual freedoms or transgressive pleasures (Fiske, 1989; Nava, 1992). The strength of the historical case argued by Nava (1996), Felski (1995), Bowlby (1985) and Reekie (1995) hinges around the social reaction to the growth and popularity of female consumption in the late nineteenth century and into the twentieth century. However, the scale of the scandal of feminine pleasures in consumption was as double-edged and ambivalent in Victorian Britain, in America and in Australia, as moral panics are today. What can be read into the titillated, exaggerated over-reactions of the male moral guardians is as much a projection of their fears and fantasies of female sexuality as it is any accurate reflection of what women are doing or thinking about as they walked around the department stores. In other words, fascinating though these accounts may be (and this includes the novels upon which many of these authors are also reliant as evidence), it is historically and sociologically debateable to construct an argument about female consumption in nineteenth-century society by relying on such limited source material.

Women's new public freedom in the new department stores, to browse and wander, to feel the luxurious textures of the silks and laces on display and to linger in the restaurants, described as it is in this context, gives us only the merest hint of the social relations entailed in these leisure practices. Shopping in the grand sense described by these authors was, at that time, for ladies of leisure. Reekie acknowledges this point without further prob-lematizing it: 'the typical drapery store customer in the nineteenth century was a middle-class or wealthy woman' (Reekie, 1995: 7). The precise history of how and where working-class women and girls did their shopping is yet to be written. And who is to say that these same middle-class women were not possibly the sort of customers for whom class antagonism was waged over the counter. Shop assistants played the same sort of role as servants. Theirs was a position of servitude (Benson, 1986). They

FEMINIST REVIEW NO 55, SPRING 1997

could be sacked on the spot for not treating the customers with the correct degree of deference. In these circumstances empowerment and authority can be (and certainly was) as much about power and authority over those deemed socially subordinate as it is (or was) about new female freedoms. This treatment by women who consider themselves socially superior is the sort of experience which anybody who has ever served in a shop has direct experience of and to have this important, indeed even formative moment of social interaction written out of feminist histories of shopping is strange to say the least. In some respects it is a way of avoiding the issue which is that these relations are not just about the neutral-sounding term class differences between women, but are actually about class antagonism. If 'we' feminists now recognize diversity within the category of women, then we must also recognize the consequences of this in terms of both class and ethnicity. Middle-class women can be as much the perpetrators of class inequalities as their male counterparts. The privileges of their social position will inevitably be manifest in those spheres in which they play a key role. Not to acknowledge this as an ongoing issue in feminist scholarship is to exculpate whole social categories of women from responsibility and agency in history on the grounds of their sex. Vron Ware has charted white women's role in the construction of empire and imperialism (Ware, 1992). But we cannot talk about middle-class women 'at home' during the same period unless we are willing to confront some of the social consequences of their status in their everyday environment.

So keen to foreground female pleasures, this work studiously ignores the production of consumption as though it did not exist. This is as true in the historical work on modernity as it is in the recent work on consumer culture. It is as though no women were employed in the low paid retail sector, as though no women worked through the night to 'finish' off the dresses and ball gowns which only a tiny few could afford, and as though no women were employed to service the consumer goods in the home as domestic servants, washing and laundering, repairing and mending, 'dressing' the mistress, looking after her wardrobe and picking her discarded clothes from the floor, i.e. providing the human service needed to allow the consumer goods to function as such.

Feminist critics argue that women as a category have been left out of the great accounts of modernity (e.g. Berman, 1982). But instead of tackling some of the more politically problematic aspects which emerge precisely from all these exclusions from modernity, exclusions without which it could not have constructed its marvellous edifices (see Gilroy, 1993a; Braidotti, 1992), some feminists have chosen to write women back into this history through a focus on consumption and the urban experience and in so doing reproduce these same evasive strategies around class and inequality. As a result at points they portray a social scenario of delights, pleasures and achievements rather than miseries and exclusions.

In retrieving a presence for middle-class women in the city and arguing this to play a role in the formation of modernity, these authors miss the opportunity of developing a fuller argument which might suggest that it was partly through the various forced exclusions of women into the domestic sphere, into the household world of shopping and into the internalized world of the sexualized body and femininity and maternity that modernity allowed itself to emerge triumphant in the public sphere as a space of white, male, reason, rationality and bureacracy. While some strata of young middle-class women could be drafted into carrying out the regulatory social work of the city, in the form of philanthropic visiting, their services were quite quickly dispensed of when it came to developing the great infrastructures of state and government.

Mica Nava suggests that Janet Wolff's (1990) argument, that women in the modernity of the late nineteenth century were not able to be 'flâneurs' because they were in the process of being removed from the public sphere of work and the urban environment into the safety of the home and the suburbs, needs to be revised to take into account the new freedom women had to browse and spend time in the department stores. (Wolff actually quite carefully qualifies her claims by emphasizing that she is concerned very much with the literary and poetic accounts which configured the flâneur as observer of modernity. She also notes the inevitable discrepancy between the ideology of domesticity and the reality of working women's lives (Wolff, 1990: 35).) Nava then reminds us of the busy lives of 'middle-class women' who 'travelled with increasing freedom through the streets and open spaces of the city' (Nava, 1996: 43). She also notes how these women 'also visited less salubrious neighbourhoods as part of the proliferation of philanthropic schemes' (Nava, 1996: 944). She continues, 'Indeed in their pursuit of "adventure, self-discovery and meaningful work" many [women] would have ventured into slum territory unfamiliar even to their husbands or brothers' (Nava, 1996: 944). While Nava does then note that 'the visonary element in their activities was perhaps somewhat compromised by the fact that their personal freedom . . . was gained in the process of trying to enforce it elsewhere, on the women of the poorer classes' (Nava, 1996: 44), my own response to this can only be polemical. If the streets were 'notorious' and full of 'disreputable strangers', who were the degraded and impoverished bodies who constituted these social categories? How was their experience of modernity? The power and privilege which allowed this minority of women such 'freedom' cannot in short be understood without taking into account the experience of those many women and girls who were the object of these concerned gazes and for

FEMINIST REVIEW NO 55, SPRING 1997

whom the city was a place of work and livelihood, who lived in 'slum territory' and who travelled about the city not because they had gained some new found freedom but as part of their everyday gainful activities. How else did working women through the centuries get to their work, run errands for their masters and mistresses, take some time for pleasure and enjoyment, and indeed escape the overcrowded conditions of their homes, but by walking about and by hanging about on the streets? Judging by some recent accounts it is as though until middle-class women tested the waters of danger by stepping foot inside a department store or by visiting the poor, the streets of the great cities like London were populated only by men. Apart from anything else this contradicts the historical evidence put forward in Sally Alexander's account of women workers in nineteenth-century London. Alexander quotes Arthur Mumby describing the flow of female labour over London Bridge in 1861 as follows:

> One meets them at every step; young women carrying large bundles of umbrella frames home to be covered; young women carrying cages full of hats, which yet want the silk and the binding, coster girls often dirty and sordid, going to fill their empty baskets, and above all female sack-makers.

(Mumby quoted in Alexander, 1976: 73)

What I am arguing is that it makes no sense at all to correct the gender blindness of writers like Berman by writing middle-class women into modernity as consumers or indeed as philanthropists (who were in the privileged position of being able to work unpaid) without also recognizing that the majority of young and old working-class women at this time had to get up at ungodly hours in the morning and walk unchaperoned to their places of work in shops, factories as well as in private homes thus making a remarkable contribution to the *workforce of modernity*. In summary it might be more useful to consider one manifestation of the productivity of power in the late nineteenth century as residing in the complex ways in which some degree of female freedom could be permitted by exacting from these women knowledge of the more dangerous classes obtained through practices of urban surveillance in the form of visiting, etc. At the same time some of these women might well have been so shocked by the poverty and suffering which they witnessed that they indeed became deeply committed to campaigning for political action and reform.

These new consumerist perspectives have emerged out of debates in media and cultural studies which have disputed the image of consumers as manipulable, passive dupes. In the analysis of contemporary consumer society, it has grown out of an awareness that the categories of social class and the traditional place occupied by the working class has undergone rapid and irreversible change in Britain over the last twenty-five years. The focus then is on how attachments to goods and to the 'social life of things' can in fact be productive of new social identities. On occasion this has allowed contemporary social and cultural theorists to leave class behind. But such social changes along with the intensification of consumption and the apparent access of ordinary people to wide ranges of consumer goods should not be used as an excuse to ignore the limits of consumption and to dismiss the work and wage needed to be able to participate in consumption. Nor should it lead to the abandonment of class as a primary concept for understanding social structure. Class, gender and ethnicity have to be continually re-interrogated for their meaning and they also have to be 'thought together'. The same goes for discussions of consumption. Since women's place in contemporary society has undergone such rapid changes it is also necessary to take these into account. If, for example, 25 per cent of the labour force in Britain now works part-time, and if 65 per cent of these workers are female, and if 42 per cent of births are to unmarried women and 1 in 3 (soon to be 1 in 2) marriages fail, and if 20 per cent of all households are currently headed by an unsupported single mother, and finally if 60 per cent of part-time workers need to rely on income support to bring their weekly income up to a so-called living wage (all figures from *Social Trends*, March 1996), then to talk in uncomplicated terms about women comprising the bulk of consumers without considering the consequences these factors have for participation in consumption, is neither politically nor intellectually viable. These figures make Lury's a conservative estimate of poverty and suggest that most women in contemporary Britain are struggling and making sacrifices to make ends meet.

Perhaps the real issue is that a good deal of the new consumerist studies remain sociologically ungrounded. With the exception of Lunt and Livingstone's social psychological study of attitudes to money and goods, savings and debt (Lunt and Livingstone, 1992), there are few detailed accounts of consumption and I am unaware of any feminist work which is looking at how women actually shop and what sort of issues influence their choices. The only material on this subject, comes, not surprisingly from the poverty lobby and from those concerned with the feminization of poverty (see Brannen and Wilson, 1987). What scanty work there is shows that women most often consume with their families' or their children's needs uppermost in their minds. Women frequently consume on behalf of others. They make personal sacrifices as a matter of course to be able to afford treats and birthday presents for their children and grandchildren. Single mothers often find themselves put under enormous pressures to compensate to their children for not having a father and hence not fulfilling the real family image which prevails in consumer culture by giving into their demands for the latest pair of trainers (Middleton, Ashworth and Walker, 1994). Indeed the phrase 'giving in' is indicative of all the conflicts and anxieties around consumption.

There is also a complete absence of the position of black and Asian women as consumers. Were this to be done it would surely point to other variables, other clusters of meaning coming into play, many of which would once again tell of memories of poverty, domestic service and of being 'on the other side of the counter'. This is not to suggest that Asian and black women only engage with consumption from the perspective of exclusion, far from it. It is simply more likely that, as with women of working-class origin, it is difficult to embrace the language of the new consumerist studies without questioning the terms of participation. Many women would not want to be understood as participating in the consumer culture with the same casual confidence as their white, middle-class counterparts. Many are (and were) not permitted to, through the subtle grids of classification and distinction which define how and where we consume. Modes of consumption thus become marks of social and cultural difference. Likewise the frustrated experience of exclusions from consumption can be a profoundly politicizing process which forces young people to confront the meaning of class, gender and ethnicity in their own homes, neighbourhoods, schools and shopping centres.

While every young black or Asian woman I have interviewed or spoken to in relation to my current research on the fashion industry (McRobbie, forthcoming) has described their relation to fashion in terms of pleasure and enjoyment they have also all referenced this interest through the language of work and labour.[4] Many of their mothers and grandmothers learnt to sew as a way of avoiding having to clean white people's houses (Wallace, 1996). Sewing and dressmaking were handed down to their daughters as useful skills which would also allow them to produce their own beautiful clothes when they could not possibly have afforded to buy them. This is borne out by the fact that most young women and men of so-called ethnic origin studying fashion design in the art schools and as far as I can ascertain all well-known black fashion designers currently working in the UK come from families where the mother and other women in the house sewed and where the kitchen and living room floors were continually covered in fabric and paper patterns and where sewing and dressmaking (whether here in the UK or else in Jamaica, in Africa or in Asia) was an ongoing household activity. Although much of this kind of domestic work is now being replaced with new cultures of consumption in the form of ready-made clothing purchasable on a global basis, it functions nonetheless as an important, even formative memory.[5]

Having described some of the problems with the new consumerist studies

I want to conclude this section by pointing in turn to some of the political weaknesses of the labour economists and sociologists whose concern is with how low paid work and exploitation provide the cheap goods for western consumers. Feminist writers like Rowbotham, Phizacklea, Tate and others have concerned themselves with the endless relocation of capital to off-shore sites and Free Trade Zones and then back to on-shore even cheaper and local sites offering low cost labour provided typically by immigrant women. They have shown how the opportunity to exploit this powerless labour force of women and children has produced the apparent buoyancy of consumer culture in fashion and in domestic goods in the west from the late 1970s. The problem lies in their reluctance to cross the divide and engage with feminists who are working at other locations in the field of consumer culture. Cultural questions including the symbolic role played by consumer goods cut no ice with these writers. In their work there can be no suggestion that the women and child labourers of these exploitative systems are or can also be participants at some level in consumption. There is certainly no hint of the fact that consumption might also bring some degree of enjoyment beyond the grim reality of earning enough to feed a family. In this respect these writers 'culturally deprive' women workers by so emphasizing 'dignity and daily bread' (Rowbotham and Mitter, 1994). As Stuart Hall has reminded us 'Everybody, including people in very poor societies whom we in the West frequently speak about as though they inhabit a world outside culture, knows that today's "goods" double up as social signs and produce meanings as well as energy' (Hall, 1989: 131).

The message which comes across from this political and intellectual lobby is to boycott all goods found to be produced in low wage, non-union factories or sweatshops. The eventual success of the recent 'anti-Gap' campaign initiated by the Labour Co-ordinating Committee of the US in 1995 was the result of intense struggle and extensive publicity drawing attention to the child labourers used to produce the cheap but high-quality cotton shirts we have come to associate with The Gap. In the end The Gap signed an agreement guaranteeing the protection of human rights to all its employees along with regular inspection of factories. However The Gap is one of thousands of successful retailers and bad publicity does not always lead to manufacturers signing agreements to introduce better working conditions. A recent documentary programme accused Marks & Spencer of exploiting child labour in South East Asia and the response of M&S was to take out a libel action against the TV company on the grounds that it never 'knowingly' employed under-age workers. In Britain, where trade unionism has been more or less decimated (with unions like USDAW barely holding onto any membership whatsoever, and that only in food retail and not at all in fashion and clothing), and where most fashion manufacturers now run strictly non-union shops, and where anyway most fashion producers work as part of a long and anonymous sub-contracting chain, dispersed across country and city, the prospect of re-unionization and even of a decent battle for a minimum wage is bleak.

There are also limits to the politics of the boycott. Hard pressed consumers will frequently return to the cheap retail outlet when the fuss has died down. This means that in broad political terms the campaigns can only play on people's consciences and as we all know battling against poverty on a global basis is an exhausting and demoralizing struggle. However, the inattention to cultural questions by the materialists and the excessive concern with culture and meaning by those in feminist cultural studies means that an opportunity for dialogue is continually averted. In addition where the materialists look in depth at the scale of exploitation with all the facts and figures at their fingertips, they remain unimpressed it seems by the arguments emerging from the field of post-colonial writing where consumer culture in the form of global communications offers new possibilities for hybridic political alliances (Gilroy, 1993b; Hall, 1996). Meanwhile cultural studies remain relatively oblivious to facts and figures and to the political role they can and do play. But even if these facts and figures are 'fictions', they are useful fictions and the extent to which current talk about consumer culture is ungrounded by sustained historical or sociological research seriously weakens the case of those who suggest the political mobilization that can be done around consumption.

Fashion Production, Fashion Consumption

My argument has been to re-integrate the study of production and consumption and to foreground not just work and employment in the production of consumption but also to take into account the changing nature of work and employment. Given that I have also been arguing for specificity and particularity it makes some sense to end this piece by making some comments about how the British fashion industry looks if we approach it from this more integrative perspective. Given that there has been a concern with political change in this piece I will also argue that indeed the only hope for both the fashion industry per se and for those women employed at each rung on the low pay ladder is to be able to think across the currently unbridgeable gap between textile production (i.e. weaving, fabric-making, etc.); manufacture and design, between sewing and sketching, between serving and being served and between working and wearing.

Fashion is of course an almost wholly feminized industry. Apart from a few men at the top, including manufacturers and retailers, celebrity designers and magazine publishers, it is and has been a female sphere of production and consumption. For this reason alone fashion *is* a feminist issue. It comprises of six component parts: manufacture and production; design; retail and distribution; education and training; the magazine and fashion media; and the practices of consumption. If we consider these one at a time, demonstrating their mutual dependence as well as their apparent distance from each other, it is possible to see a set of tensions and anxieties which in turn provide opportunities for political debate and social change. Thinking across the fashion sector in this way also has the advantage of disaggregating what often seem like a series of starkly monolithic institutions. Given the scale and the power of the huge multi-nationals which create the conditions for consumer culture in the west it is often difficult to see a political light at the end of the tunnel, and perhaps it is for this reason that the new consumerist writers place so much emphasis on the subversive things people can do with consumer goods.

Let us look then, briefly at manufacture and production. Phizacklea has already shown that factory production in this country is a sunset industry and the only on-shore activity of any significance comprises of the small sub-contracted units of production often headed by small-scale ethnic entrepreneurs themselves seeking a livelihood in fashion manufacture as an alternative to unemployment (Phizacklea, 1990). The women workers in this sector receive very low pay and are often also homeworkers. There is no significant union recognition nor any likelihood of it. However gloomy though this may seem, self-organization of homeworkers is not unimaginable, as Tate has shown (Tate, 1994). There is no reason why the highly skilled knitters described recently in *The Independent* as supplying the top fashion designers should not find ways of improving their working conditions and their wages (*The Independent*, 24 February 1996). Publicity, lobbying and support from other sectors of the industry including the powerful fashion magazines (and so-called celebrity politics) could achieve a lot in a short space of time. The recent Oxfam Clothes Code campaign has, for example, drawn on figures like comedienne Jo Brand to persuade all retailers to adhere to a code of conduct guaranteeing decent working conditions in all their factories across the world. This sector could also put pressure on government to support further training and education which would allow women to move into better paid and more highly skilled work, as pattern cutters, for example (where there is a skill shortage) and it would also allow them to cut out the middlemen and subcontractors who currently negotiate all costs and take comfortable percentages. Finally this strategy would also allow the low paid women to get closer to the designers and retailers who at present they never see and often don't even know they are working for. British fashion designers typically work on a small scale self-employed basis. Even well-known names frequently employ fewer than twenty people direct. There is no inherent reason why closer collaboration of this sort could not take place to the mutual advantage of all parties.

Education and training would also have a role to play in this more collaborative strategy. At present fashion design education is too committed to defending the fine art status of fashion to be interested at all in manufacture and production. As a feminine field in the high-culture-oriented world of the art schools, fashion design educators have looked up towards the fine arts for legitimation. But this is helpful neither to the industry as a whole nor to the young fashion design students themselves for whom it is often a mark of professional pride *not* to know how to put in a zip (astonishing though this may be to the outside world; see McRobbie, forthcoming). The vast majority of fashion students never visit a factory throughout their degree. In some ways it is convenient to them not to have to know about how orders are actually put into production and who actually makes them since this would raise the unpleasant question of what sort of wages they are being paid and what sort of working conditions they are being expected to put up with. As one fashion academic said to me, 'It would take all the romance out of it for them.' But not knowing about production and manufacture is also unhelpful to the graduates in the longer term. It leaves them open to exploitation by unscrupulous suppliers and middlemen who over-charge them while massively under-paying their sub-contracted women workers. It means in short that fashion designers don't have the kind of grasp of the industry as a whole that they should have. It is not inconceivable however that at some point with more realistic education and training, young designers might work on a more equal basis with the women who do the sewing and finishing. All it would take would be more open public debate on the fashion industry and also on the unviability of designers making a livelihood for themselves without thoroughly involving themselves at every stage in production and manufacture. Fashion educators, the great majority of whom are women, would also have a clear role to play in this respect.

The designers themselves, most of whom are working in the shadow of unemployment and are or have been dependent on government sponsored schemes like the Enterprise Allowance Scheme and other benefits, might also recognize what they have in common with other women working throughout the industry. The class divide between them and the machinists is not as great as it might seem. Many have mothers who have worked in the industry. In addition fashion designers are as likely to exploit themselves as they are to employ an exploited workforce, so there is a good deal of work of de-mystification and de-glamorization to be done in this respect.

The final three parts of the industry, the magazines, retail and consumption, would also need to be re-conceptualized along the same lines. Fashion magazines at present have a foolish and unnecessry commitment to avoiding serious or political issues. But this might change. Young women fashion journalists might at some point be willing to persuade their editors that a piece on the exploited labour that goes into a designer dress might be worthy of a few pages. Instead of supporting the fashion industry by producing gushy pages of praise for the work of the new crop of British designers, the magazines could take this kind of risk. Likewise retail workers might recognize themselves to have more in common with other workers in the fashion industry than with those employed in selling food or furniture or whatever. Anyway, given the virtually non-existent rate of trade unionization in this sector, new forms of organization and collaboration would need to be established. Fashion retail staff identify strongly with fashion and less with retail, but they are now employed on short-term, part-time contracts, often they are working largely for commission. Their self-image as working in the glamorous fashion industry must surely be undercut by the reality of knowing that in a few years time possibly with children to support it is unlikely that they would hold onto the job of decorating the shopfloor at Donna Karan. What sort of long-term career is there in fashion retail? At present nobody knows because no research has been done on this side of shopping. Research and public debate would be a useful way of beginning to improve the conditions of women who work in this sector.

This leaves us with the practices of consumption. If consumers were to be thoroughly alerted to the inhumane activities which eventually bring clothes to the rails of many of the department stores in the way that the politics of food production has made some impact on food consumption then pressure might also be brought to bear by consumer organizations for changes in the fashion industry. Many women and girls already deeply object to the 200 per cent (at least) mark up on items of fashion. They know how little the women who produce the clothes get paid and frequently the consumers vote with their feet and look but don't buy, even if they could afford to. The fashion industry knows this to be the case but is at present incapable of thinking reflexively about its own practices. A (New) Labour policy which realistically recognized the British fashion industry as a place of many people's livelihoods and also as a potential site for providing more work on a more secure basis on the longer term, instead of seeing it as a piece of light entertainment, might be better able to translate the desires of many women, including young women, to make a good living in fashion. Often it is through consuming that women want to become producers. The energetic enthusiasm of women across the boundaries of class and ethnicity for fashion could be used to transform it into a better place of work rather than allowing it to remain a space of exploited production and guilty consumption.

FEMINIST REVIEW NO 55, SPRING 1997

Notes

Angela McRobbie teaches Sociology at Loughborough University. Thanks to Andrew Ross for inviting me to deliver a version of this paper at the Fashion Victims; Labour, Spectacle and Policy Conference held at New York University in March 1996.

1 Some upmarket fashion shops in London now employ doormen/security guards who can stop people from entering if they do not look as though they have the money to buy. They do this by saying that 'the shop is too busy right now', even though it is quite clear to the would-be customers that the shop is in fact relatively empty.

2 These political positions could be broadly characterized as traditional socialist-feminism in contrast to variations of the new post-feminism which also embrace so-called identity politics.

3 The same argument could be made in relation to recent discussions of the 'pink pound'. What is missing here are the working conditions (i.e. behind the bar) of those mostly young gay men who service this industry. What sort of career is it? What are the pay and conditions?

4 This research has involved extensive interviews with young British fashion designers with a view to building up a picture of employment in the creative and cultural sectors.

5 I count myself in this category since my own grandmother was a skilled tailoress from Dublin who emigrated to Glasgow in 1915. My own early childhood memories are of her living room floor scattered with pieces of paper patterns and bits of fabric.

References

ALEXANDER, Sally (1976) 'Women's work in 19thC London' in **Mitchell,** and **Oakley,** editors *The Rights and Wrongs of Women* Harmondsworth: Penguin.

BENSON, Susan Porter (1986) *Counter Cultures: Saleswomen, Managers and Customers in American Department Stores 1890–1940* Urbana: University of Illinois Press.

BERMAN, Marshall (1982) *'All That Is Solid Melts Into Air': The Experience of Modernity* London: Verso.

BOWLBY, Rachel (1985) *Just Looking: Consumer Culture in Dreiser, Gissing and Zola* London: Methuen.

BRAIDOTTI, Rosi (1992) 'On the feminist female subject or from she-self to she-other' in **Bock** and **James,** editors *Beyond Equality and Difference: Citizenship, Feminist Politics and Female Subjectivity* London: Routledge.

BRANNEN, Julia and **WILSON, Gail** (eds) (1987) *Give and Take in Families.* London: Allen & Unwin.

FELSKI, Rita (1995) *The Gender of Modernity* London and Cambridge, MA: Harvard University Press.

FISKE, John (1989) *Understanding Popular Culture* London: Unwin Hyman.

GILROY, Paul (1993a) *The Black Atlantic: Modernity and Double Consciousness* London: Verso.

GILROY, Paul (1993b) *Small Acts* London: Serpents Tail.

HALL, Stuart (1989) 'The meaning of new times' in **Hall** and **Jacques**, editors *New Times: The Changing Face of Politics in the 1990s* London: Lawrence & Wishart.

HALL, Stuart (1996) 'New ethnicities' in **Morley** and **Chen**, editors *Stuart Hall: Critical Dialogues in Cultural Studies* London: Routledge.

LUNT, Peter and LIVINGSTONE, Sonia (1992) *Mass Consumption and Personal Identity: Everyday Economic Experience* Buckingham: Open University Press.

LURY, Celia (1996) *Consumer Culture* Oxford: Polity Press.

McROBBIE, Angela (forthcoming) *Fashion and the Image Industries* London: Routledge.

MIDDLETON, Sue, ASHWORTH, Karl and WALKER, Robert (1994) *Family Fortunes: The Pressures on Parents and Children in the 1990s* London: Child Poverty Action Group.

MORT, Frank (1989) 'The politics of consumption' in **Hall** and **Jacques**, editors *New Times: The Changing Face of Politics in the 1990s* London: Lawrence & Wishart.

MORT, Frank (1996) *Cultures of Consumption* London: Routledge.

NAVA, Mica (1992) *Changing Cultures: Feminism, Youth and Consumerism* London: Sage.

NAVA, Mica (1996) 'Modernity's disavowal: women, the city, and the department store' in **Nava** and **O'Shea**, editors *Modern Times: Reflections on a Century of English Modernity* London: Routledge.

PHIZACKLEA, Annie (1990) *Unpacking the Fashion Industry: Gender, Racism and Class in Production* London: Routledge.

PUMPHREY, Martin (1987) 'The flapper, the housewife and the making of modernity' *Cultural Studies* Vol. 1, No. 2: 179–93.

REEKIE, Gail (1995) *Temptations: Sex, Selling and the Department Store* Sydney: Allen & Unwin.

ROWBOTHAM, Sheila and MITTER, Swasti (eds) (1994) *Dignity and Daily Bread: New Forms of Economic Organising Among Poor Women in the Third World and the First* London: Routledge.

Social Trends (1996) London: HMSO.

TATE, Jane (1994) 'Homework in West Yorkshire' in **Rowbotham** and **Mitter**, editors.

WILLIAMS, Sally (1996) 'The designer jumper you're wearing: where did it come from?' *The Independent*, 24 February.

WALLACE, Michelle (1996) 'Fashion consumption' paper delivered at Fashion Victims Conference, New York University March.

WARE, Vron (1992) *Beyond the Pale: White Women, Racism and History* London: Verso.

WOLFF, Janet (1990) *Feminine Sentences: Essays on Women and Culture* Cambridge: Polity Press.

LIBERTY

SUCCESS

STATUS

WEALTH

LIBERTY

SUCCESS

STATUS

'Desperately Seeking . . .'

ROMANCE

LOVE

ROMANCE

HAPPINESS

Joy Gregory

Looking Good:

The Lesbian Gaze and Fashion Imagery

Reina Lewis

FEMINIST REVIEW NO 55, SPRING 1997, pp. 92–109

Abstract

This paper is concerned with the different forms of pleasure and identification activated in the consumption of dominant and subcultural print media. It centres on
an analysis of the lesbian visual pleasures generated through the reading of fashion
editorial in the new lesbian and gay lifestyle magazines. This consideration of the
lesbian gaze is contrasted to the lesbian visual pleasures obtained from an against
the grain reading of mainstream women's fashion magazines. The development of
the lesbian and gay lifestyle magazines, in the context of the pink pound, produces
a situation in which an eroticized lesbian visual pleasure is the overt remit of the
magazine, rather than a clandestine pleasure obtained through a transgressive
reading of dominant cultural imagery. In contrast to the polysemic free-play of
fashion fantasy by which readers produce lesbian pleasure in the consumption of
mainstream magazines, responses to the fashion content in the lesbian magazine
Diva suggest that in a subcultural context readers deploy a realist mode of reading
that demands a monosemic positive images iconography. The article uses the
concept of subcultural competency to consider the different ways lesbians read
mainstream and subcultural print media and suggests that the conflict over *Diva*'s
fashion spreads may be linked to changing patterns of identification and the use of
dress for recognizability.

Keywords

lesbian; fashion; gaze; consumption; lifestyle

Introduction

One of the results of the growth and recognition of the pink economy in
the late 1980s was the establishment of a number of lesbian and gay 'lifestyle' magazines in the UK and North America in the early 1990s (this
would include in the UK *Diva*, *Attitude*, *Phase*, and in USA and Canada,
Out, *Girlfriends*, *Curve*, formally *Deneuve*). Although they often had some
overtly political content (from articles on lesbian mothers to coverage of
Pride) these journals did not see lesbian and gay or queer identities only in
political terms. In contrast to previous campaigning journals, the new titles
mixed politics and consumption in a move that was in keeping with the

new recognition of the pink pound (whose advertising revenue was crucial to them). More and more mainstream and gay-run businesses realized the potential of extending 1980s niche marketing techniques to include gay and, to a lesser extent, lesbian consumers (Clark, 1993). As Frank Mort has demonstrated, this increase in consumer possibilities meant that lesbian and gay individuals grew increasingly familiar with the idea that consumption itself marked out ways of participating in a gay life (Mort, 1996). The emphasis on lifestyle in these magazines was part of this formation.

I am interested here in how readers consume the magazines, particularly in the ways in which lesbians consume the fashion coverage in *Diva* (with some comparison to other journals and to gay male readers). Looking at fashion allows me to think about the specificity of a lesbian visual pleasure and forms of identification in an area of cultural consumption traditionally aimed at women. Previously, with Katrina Rolley, I had analysed how lesbians could extract visual pleasures from mainstream fashion magazines such as *Vogue* and *Elle* (Lewis and Rolley, 1996). In this article I want to extend that discussion to consider what happens when fashion, with all its expected pleasures, moves to a venue where same-sex pleasure is the overt rather than covert remit of the publication.

For lesbian magazines, which often inherited a feminist perspective, the inclusion of fashion was a conspicuous departure from previous feminist publications, whose opposition to the fashion industry is legendary. But it was not only a greater adherence to feminist politics that separated out lesbian and gay magazines: the economic base that supported the new commercialized lifestyles and identities was unequal too. As Mort points out, the power of the pink pound was mainly seen as male – with far fewer services aimed at lesbians – and the mode of metropolitan gay life inscribed in the pink and style press relied on (and created opportunities for), shops and bars that mainly catered for male markets. Lesbians, who as women often, but not always, have less (disposable) income, were inevitably seen as a bad financial bet. So the opportunities for advertising, commercial tie-ins, etc. in *Diva* were far less. The new identification-as-consumption model of the pink pound was not embraced by all and to some extent the feminist politics of *Diva* produced an ambivalent attitude to the pink pound's valorization of shopping.

The different consumer habits assumed in lesbians and gay men (which also determine the magazine's access to clothes for fashion editorial) as well as their reading of the fashion images can be related to their different historical relationships to fashion. Whilst lesbians have in recent decades invested heavily in an anti-fashion and anti-consumerism politics and aesthetics – now under review with the advent of the lipstick lesbian – gay men have historically marked out their identity through sartorial savvy, ritualized consumption and investment in a discourse of taste. Whatever the vogue for 'real' men or dressing down, gay men's magazines do not have to overcome an antipathy to the very idea of fashion in the way that a lesbian and particularly a feminist lesbian publication does. But, whatever the attitude to fashion, dress as a marker of identity is hugely significant in the everyday lives of lesbians and gay men: clothes function as a marker of recognizability to other gays or as a method of passing (which may itself be gay-coded for those in the know, whilst safely enough secured as heterosexual for those to whom one cannot risk being known). Moreover, as consumers of each others' appearance, there is a pleasure to be had in recognizing and being recognized. For these reasons, clothes have an importance in the lives of lesbians and gays – whether or not they consider themselves fashionable – that is rarely experienced by heterosexuals, however much they may affiliate to alternative networks of style and subcultural identities (on the related passings of sexual and racialized identifications see Walker, 1993).

But, new departure as their fashion pages may have been, the lesbian lifestyle magazines were not starting with a blank slate. Although fashion was rarely seen on the pages of *Spare Rib*, many lesbians had been reading mainstream fashion magazines for years, without forgetting their lesbian selves as they turned the page. As Katrina and I argued, fashion editorial in mainstream magazines regularly used visual codes that foregrounded the possibility of a lesbian visual pleasure (see also Clark, 1993). These codes typically broke down into four sections: images which reference era/locales known to have lesbian historical significance (Brassai's Paris or Vita Sackville West-style English country homes); gendered coupling of female models where they take on a male/female dynamic; or cross-dressing where female models take on male codes; and twinning or mirroring. This reading is based on a recognition that the fundamental contradiction of female magazine consumption – in which women are tutored in looking at, admiring and identifying with other women's bodies – is a potentially eroticized experience for all women readers, not just lesbians. The fashion magazine is widely understood to be a world without men, yet one that is animated by them. Men's conspicuous absence from fashion imagery is in direct relation to their presumed central role in the lives of the female addressee of the magazine: it is for 'his' eyes that the magazines' consumers study the arts of beauty and dress.

It was part of my argument in that piece that the lesbian viewer is engaged in a mode of narcissistic identification with the beautiful woman in the image which – relying on the implicit awareness of other lesbian viewers who, like her, gaze at the beautiful woman – produces a desire both to be and to have the displayed woman. As I gaze at the model, I may simultaneously at a fantasy level desire to be like her, and desire to have her and, moreover, desire to be, as she is, the recipient of another woman's desiring gaze. Further, in the 'all female' world of the fashion magazine, the logic of a female desiring gaze produces what I call a paradigmatically lesbian viewing position for any woman, whether or not she is consciously lesbian identified. The tradition of an overtly heterosexual rationale in the magazine world plus the commonplace trivialization of fashion (see Evans and Thornton, 1989) recoups this subversive position to the point where it is quite clearly not an uncomfortable experience for a heterosexual viewer to gaze at female flesh in this way. She can, after all, imagine that she is looking at them in order to learn how to make herself that desirable for her man. (For a different reading of mainstream magazines' invocation and disavowal of a lesbian reading position, see Fuss, 1992.) But it does not police against lesbian pleasure.

It is clear that one of the elements that animated this analysis was the idea of imagined interpretive communities of other lesbians. We were thinking of reception in social terms, in which the psychic mechanisms of fantasy activated by the viewing experience are also socially structured. In this instance, the experience of pleasure seemed to rest on recognizable lesbian visual codes and on the activity of a transgressive, and often narrativized, reading. But what happens when that reading is not transgressive, when a same-sex narrative is the denoted, not the connoted, of the text?

Theorizing the reader of lesbian and gay lifestyle journalism

Now that we had overtly 'lesbian' fashion pages, how much did the putative lesbian 'we' like what we saw? The 'we' who looks is very important. Meaning does not reside in the image itself, but is generated in the interaction between viewer and text in which the codes of the text will be more or less decipherable to different viewers, depending on their historical and cultural moment. In this case, I need to be clear that there is no such thing as 'the' lesbian gaze, singular; since all lesbians are differentiated by class and racializing terms. But we can recognize the impact of such larger formations as subcultural groupings within which the individual lesbian subject may sometimes identify.

Caroline Evans and Lorraine Gamman also make a case for the importance of what they call subcultural competencies (Evans and Gamman, 1995). These are what make the lesbian viewer able, for example, to recognize the lesbian subcultural referents and cross-gendered lesbian erotics connoted by a 'Napoleon and Josephine' narrative in *Vogue Italia* (where two women maintain an eroticized butch/femme dynamic sumptuously styled as the historical pair in a suitably lush and imperial setting). Evans and Gamman emphasize that the pleasure apparently produced by the code under discussion does not reside *in* the representation, but in the activity of decoding it. In other words, it is the act of interpretation itself that is eroticized, driven in part by the thrill of detecting a lesbian pleasure in the mainstream location. This means that there is no such thing as a pre-ordained lesbian gaze, so much as a gaze that is able to decode lesbian sub-cultural referents, variable and shifting as they are: it is the exercise of a subcultural competency that produces lesbian pleasure, a pleasure that would be available to anyone able to exercise a similar competency whether lesbian or not (Evans and Gamman, 1995: 35).

This for them can apply equally to the reading of dominant or subcultural texts. I am concerned with the specificities of each: in the case of a 'dominant' text like *Vogue* I absolutely agree that the eroticization comes via the exercise of a subcultural competency. But this pleasure is heightened into a thrill by the sense of transgression that comes from constructing an alternative narrative. In the case of lesbian magazines, where the same sub-culturally recognizable codes are the denoted rather than the connoted of the text, they read differently and sometimes, I think, produce less visual pleasure. Context is all.

This may be in part due to production values (money on the page) which in the case of smaller lesbian and gay magazines struggling to get advertising are generally much lower than the mainstream glossies. The high cost luxury mise-en-scène that is part of the visual pleasure of mainstream fashion coverage is absent from most lesbian and gay products such as *Diva* or free papers, *Boyz*, or the *Pink*. One exception to this is the British gay magazine *Attitude* which is notable for its glossy and gorgeous fashion editorial and is generally more visual-led (in keeping with previous staff experience on the now defunct gay journal *Square Peg*, which was known for its visuals). At this point, I should also report that of the cluster of titles available in the UK in 1994 (*Shebang*, *Phase*, *Diva*, *Attitude*) only half have survived, and they have only been running for two years. So I want to signal both the newness of the field (magazines are still trying things out and establishing a sense of their readership) and the methodological implications of trying to make deductions from such a small field. This places a terrible burden of representation on my sample, especially when compared to our earlier sample from the mainstream media where we were able to analyse five titles over ten years. So this piece is necessarily rather more exploratory in nature: my comparisons of British and American, and lesbian and gay and mixed magazines, can only be suggestive at this stage.

Figure 1 *Crossover Images.* **Photograph: Simon Pattle**

Although I am primarily talking about lesbian visual pleasure the comparison with mixed and gay magazines can be illuminating. It has been much documented that in recent years the male body has been objectified in popular culture in ways that were previously thought to be associated with the female body alone. As Mark Simpson discusses, all of this illustrates an increasing willingness on the part of mainstream popular culture to flirt with homoerotic pleasures (Simpson, 1994). Gay lifestyle magazines do it in reverse: in seeking to sell homosexuality as lifestyle they overtly celebrate their readers' participation in mainstream culture (as consumers if nothing else), rather than speaking to them in a cocoon of fantasized gay separation.

This means that essential advertising revenue is possible; especially as more and more mainstream advertising campaigns look increasingly at home in a gay venue. I always thought that this advert for vodka (bottom right, Figure 1) was homoerotically charged, but once seen in *Attitude* it looks just perfect for the gay bedroom wall. So, when we look at the editorial fashion coverage in gay lifestyle magazines we are viewing in the context of the increased queering of popular culture (Simpson, 1994) plus the crossover of queer-inflected representations into the queer space of the magazine itself. This raises questions about preferred and alternative meanings. During the single reading experience of flicking through a lesbian or gay magazine, viewers are engaged in reading dominant representational codes which may be more or less overtly open to same-sex pleasures (whether it is a vodka advert or a publicity shot of kd lang on the cover of *Diva*) and in reading editorial images that have an overtly gay 'meaning'. To consume a lesbian or gay lifestyle magazine is thus an experience of reading simultaneously with and against the grain, and of re-reading previously consumed images that, like the vodka advert in *Attitude*, are now overlaid with overtly homoerotic connotations in their new gay context. But one of the things that marks out *Diva* as different from *Attitude* is that it gets far less mainstream advertising and hence revenue. In keeping with the prevalent assumption that lesbians never have any money to spend, very few mainstream advertising campaigns use *Diva*. Mainstream advertising only comes *Diva*'s way when a specifically lesbian audience is sought (for example, adverts for the pop group the Buffalo Girls and for the film *Carrington*). But not always even then: the lesbian market for kd lang's 1995 album was so obviously secure that the record company decided no wooing was necessary and refused *Diva* an advert or an interview.

Diva does of course carry a mix of advertising and editorial content. But the relationship of the fashion editorial to this mix of copy seems different from the image of a complex and highly sophisticated reading practice, revelling in contradiction in a properly queer and, at times, postmodern way that the other gay magazines construct and/or welcome. *Phase*'s first spread included a tongue-in-cheek homage to lesbian chic (top right, Figure 1), reproduced from *Out* magazine USA. This not only highlights the role of consumption as a gay activity, but also invites the *Phase* reader to identify themselves as one who will recognize the iconic nature of the popular cultural examples of lesbian chic on display. In contrast, *Diva* got a mixed response to its fashion coverage.

Founded in 1994, *Diva* initially included fashion spreads but has dropped them temporarily from its contents. Editor Frances Williams anticipated that her audience would to some extent apply a realist mode of consumption, so her decision to use ethnically diverse models and 'real' people was not motivated by her own preferences alone. This was coupled with an intent to introduce a greater diversity of lesbian images into what she thought had become a rather stale iconography. Although some readers responded positively to the fashion pages, I was surprised at the level of complaints they generated: in nearly every case this was based on a realist mode of reception. Criticism centred on the non-representativeness of the models; the problems of objectification; the apparent unsuitability of the clothes featured for accepted/stereotypical/easily recognizable lesbian styles; and the cost of the clothes. Yet, presumably, some of the readers of *Diva* also read *Vogue* and are used to a non-literal consumption of fashion spreads. A feature on lesbian club promoters and bar staff reveals not only their own style choices but also their overview of the increasing fashion literacy and range of options on the lesbian scene (albeit in London only). Their comments suggest that for some lesbians the move away from a style orthodoxy is potentially liberating and some readers did indeed welcome the inclusion of fashion. But, the level of negative feedback did leave me wondering what happens to the critical faculties of readers when faced with a lesbian mis-en-scène, considering that they must also read some sort of mainstream imagery against the grain, even if not specifically fashion imagery?

My suspicion that readers have different expectations of gay-produced imagery is borne out by Murray Healy's observation that the gay free papers *Pink* and *Boyz* got complaints when the men they pictured were not standard 'real man' beefcake. As Healy observes, if you want challenging, alternative images of masculinity go to *L'Uomo Vogue* not to the gay press.[1] Again, a positive images iconography is demanded. It seems that some lesbian and gay readers demand unambiguous politically or aesthetically 'safe' images in the gay press whereas they revel in transgressive, contradictory and subversive pleasures in the mainstream. If the exercise of subcultural competencies in the reading of the dominant is eroticized through a relationship of power and knowledge (I know something 'they' don't), why is this pleasure sacrificed in the consumption of gay/subcultural texts? And in what ways is this situation different for lesbian and gay readers? Where the lesbian demand for positive images, though in itself a fantasy of representability and wholeness, is based on the possibility of literal identification, the 'real' man demanded in *Boyz* is implicitly understood as a central fantasy of subcultural iconography. So whilst both lesbian readers of *Diva* and gay readers of *Boyz* are demanding an impossible monovalency of the image, they do it in quite distinct ways.

This anxiety about the polysemic nature of imagery in the consumption of the subcultural is at odds with a homoerotic reading of the dominant which relies on the multivalency of the image for the possibility of a queer pleasure. Is the readers' desire for closure in *Diva* something that is anchored in the codes of *Diva*'s imagery, or is it brought to the images by the readers, i.e. in opposition to the magazines's preferred reading? Why, when the advent of *Diva* coincides with a dramatic change in lesbian style, do its fashion pages get a hard time, in contrast to the evidently thriving fashion content at *Attitude*, whose reception is quite different again from that of *Boyz*?

Figure 2 *Naughty but Nice*. **Photograph: Simon Pattle.**

Style counsel: fashion, reading and identification in *Diva*

One of the first spreads in *Diva* was entitled 'Naughty but nice' (Figure 2).
Here the 'naughty' overtly refers to the devilish horns worn by the models.
But it also suggests that the revealing clothes may themselves be naughty.
Yet, when we turn the page to discover the 'nice' we find a far less demure
picture: maintaining sexualized body contact at all times the two models
are now in a rougher, dykier, street-style, posing with an in-your-face know-
ingness for the camera. On one level this suggests a carnivalesque reversal,
in which the grotesque of the lesbian body is inverted as 'nice', whilst something approximating 'proper' femininity is demonized as 'naughty'. This
might be called the magazine's preferred reading, in which an audience
assumed to have lesbian subcultural competencies would decode the visual
pun of the title. But the spread offers another reading that, rather than prob-
lematizing the very idea of a binary divide by ridiculing its constituent terms,
re-naturalizes the dichotomy by presenting a lesbian binarism in which the
more masculine, dyke-referential style of the 'nice' is normatized, whilst
the femmier, mainstream fashion of the 'naughty' is presented as sub-
culturally transgressive. Although all the clothes are from a London

designer shop, the styling of the 'nice' is quite easily recognizable as a lesbianized version of what was a current club look. The jeans, the leather trousers and big leather belts cut against the cutesy T-shirts and the baby blue satin of the jacket, securing a lesbian-coding for those in the know. But both images are presented as potentially desirable for the reader.

In the following edition we see a composite of the naughty/nice narrative ('Subscribe', Figure 2). This provides a recognizable lesbian coding alongside a signification of up-to-the-minute style and awareness about lesbian dress debates, as well as a parodic but still effectively eroticized assertion of active lesbian desire. The top figure's gaze out at the viewer (a look that is echoed in the main spread) invites identification and participation. The luscious cleavage at the bottom of the frame is de-objectified (in the pejorative sense) through the model's ownership of her self-display, signified by the parodic performance of ecstasy and re-affirmed by the playful surround of the other horned figure. It is precisely the multiplicity of referents in this image (satyrs, cherubs, dykes, postmodern self-referential butch-femme) that makes it so potentially pleasurable *and* that helps it to overcome the anticipated qualms of those sections of *Diva*'s readership assumed to be concerned about the objectification of the female body. In this, it is clear that the visual language of the fashion spreads is determined to a significant extent by the editor, stylist and photographer's sense of the attitudes of their readers. Some of this may be informed by direct feedback on *Diva* (letters, questionnaires), or based on indirect (word of mouth) reader-response, or come tangentially through hearing responses to images outside the pages of the magazine. In all these ways, is their sense of the imaginary boundaries in which they operate constructed.

My sense of *Diva*'s readers is based on conversations with the editor, with women I know who read it, and on the response of non-magazine readers to whom I have shown the photographs. The differing attitudes I saw and heard to dress, desire and the role of reading in the formation of identity suggest two distinct but potentially overlapping modes of reception. One regards lesbianism as an authentic identity based on lived experience outside the magazine which readers expect *Diva* to properly reflect and represent. This identity is often predicated on the separation from and resistance to dominant models of heterosexual femininity, frequently signified by a refusal of mainstream women's fashion. The other constructs identity *through* reading and *then* seeks social spaces in which that identity can be lived out and recognized, often through the appropriation of mainstream women's fashion.

For this second group, the sense of community engendered by the magazine is paramount. The selective use of mainstream fashion fosters an identity

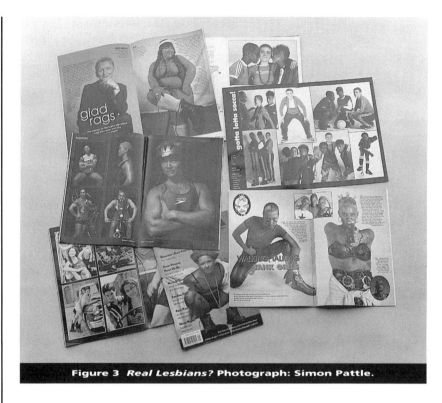

Figure 3 *Real Lesbians?* **Photograph: Simon Pattle.**

that is initially shared with an imagined interpretive community of readers and then developed experientially in social spaces (like clubs) with others who can decode it. Although the potential to be decoded by others is obviously key, it seems that this type of reader is able to deal both with the swift changes of style and fragmented identifications associated with postmodernity and with the fact that they may not be recognizable. It is no coincidence that these dress codes and senses of identity are predominantly associated with younger women whose sense of self has been formed in a different and less oppositional relationship to the media than previous generations.

Diva obviously needs to appeal to both sets of readers. In the 'Gotta Lotta Socca' spread (top right, Figure 3) the play with imagery has gone: recognizability is key. So, in this spread the subcultural referents are dominant. This, along with the 'real' looking models, produces something almost ethnographic in its documentation of an enshrined (British) lesbian icon: the footballing dyke. In magazine terms, the 'Socca' spread – with its awkward models and patent lack of artifice – is more akin to a lesbian version of teen magazines' 'readers in shopping malls' or to low-brow women's magazines like *Bella* than to high fashion fantasy. Although 'Socca' offers a significant consumer opportunity (buying football strips/sportswear is never cheap) it is clearly not exhorting its readers to enter fancy boutiques in the way that even the 'nice' was earlier. Rather, the football spread facilitates the living out of a more traditionally subcultural lesbian identity through the experience of buying men's clothes in the mainly male domain of the football sports emporium. This potential for resistance is not so simply available in the environs of a trendy fashion shop where almost anything will go.

Although the footballers might be great role models, their anti-erotic becomes even more pronounced in contrast to the presentation of the athlete's impressive physique (centre left, Figure 3). This is not because footballers are not eroticized as objects of lesbian desire: indeed they are. But the imputation of an eroticized relationship between them becomes impossible once they must symbolize a resisting subcultural position that is founded on a refusal to join in the 'patriarchal' objectification of women's bodies. In other words, they have simultaneously to be beyond recuperation by a male voyeuristic gaze and to be objects of desire for a lesbian reader. But this must be coded in a classed and masculinized style of adrogyny that has typically been resistant to an overtly eroticized objectification (not least because this is seen as implicitly femininizing) in ways that may not apply to femmier personae (which may often be more overtly presented for erotic contemplation). The awkwardness with which the 'Socca' models respond to their physical proximity looks authentic, not staged, and seems to be born out in the difficulty of this quandary. But it may also speak to a butch occupation of space, the visual pleasures of which are beyond my recuperation, since one of my 'respondents' did find the 'Socca' spread sexy. So, what different sorts of reader pleasure and/or identification do these different spreads produce? Is the blokey mateyness of the footballers condusive to a butch identification and pleasure where the parodic glamour of 'naughty but nice' is not?

I think that one of the pleasures of *Diva* is the assumed authenticity of the models. They are always identified by name, and in some cases are constructed as the authentic owners of the style they model. The 'Tank Girl' models (bottom right, Figure 3) are thanked as fans, further emphasizing the documentary nature of the feature. It is the magazine's policy to use only lesbian models and photographers, driven in part by a feminist desire to provide work for women and lesbians, but also by the pragmatic analysis that it is harder to get 'straight' models to snuggle up realistically for the camera. This brings me back to the subcultural competencies that were in operation in the consumption of *Vogue*. If *Diva* does not identify the models as lesbian, how is the reader expected to know? In part it can be explained by the bodies which are not stereotypically perfect and the determined representation of a variety of ethnicities, that draws attention to a politicized affirmative action aesthetic (even as it may activate codes

FEMINIST REVIEW NO 55, SPRING 1997

that eroticize the 'exoticism' of ethnic difference). Mainstream magazines do periodically use 'real' women or non-stereotypically beautiful models, but the exceptional nature of these instances signals their deviation from the normal rule. The out lesbian model Jenny Shimizu is an interesting case in point here: her visible ethnicity (in a world where white does not register as ethnic) and intertextually decodable lesbianism, via interviews and features, make her an exotically different visual spectacle which can be effectively contrasted with other model bodies and personae. It also signifies an up-to-the-minute association with fashionable lesbian chic. The fact that she presents as a butch dyke and not a glamour femme only re-inforces her authenticity and heightens the transgressive appeal of using a lesbian model who deviates not only from the norm but also from the over-exposed media creature of the (femme) lipstick lesbian of lesbian chic (see also O'Sullivan, 1994).

But the details of dress, hair and the relations between the pictured women in magazines such as *Diva* are also important, as is the quality of the gaze directed out of the frame towards the reader. I may not get as much pleasure from these as I do from *Vogue*, but I am never in any doubt about their lesbian address. They position me as a lesbian addressee, producing a position of empathy and also of desire. Whilst, for a generation of women reared on the icon of the unobtainable supermodel, the very approachability of these models may be their downfall, as the magazine's lesbian addressee it is their reality-effect that draws me in. Would this be legible to a reader without the appropriate subcultural competencies?

I feel in many ways that the *Diva* spreads grapple with the same problem as do my friends and I; how to look fashionable and move with the changing trends, whilst still signifying as lesbian? At one time it was relatively easy: you wore whatever you wanted and combined it with big shoes or boots. But then everyone started wearing Doc. Martens and footwear's lesbian coding was undermined. Now it is harder, plus there is a whole generation of lesbians who do not have the same agenda about recognizability and who share a dress aesthetic that owes more to the mainstream than to feminist stylistics. The outrage caused by *Diva*'s foray into disparate styles may attest to a struggle over meaning that is lived out through representation and the consumption of material culture.

'We're here, we're queer and we're not going shopping'??: Representing queerness in other lifestyle magazines

In contrast to *Diva*, *Attitude* can play with a male relationship to fashion that is clearly eroticized and fantastic and can, presumably, draw on what Mort identifies as the homosocial spaces and reading habits previously

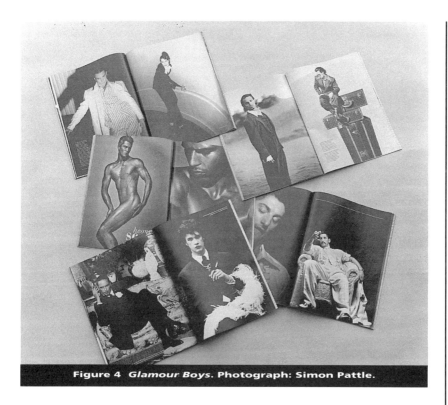

Figure 4 *Glamour Boys*. **Photograph: Simon Pattle.**

constructed by the men's style press of the 1980s (Mort, 1996). There is little recourse to authenticity or documentary in these examples from *Attitude* (Figure 4). The splendour of the dressed male figure is more closely akin to the unobtainable glamour of the supermodel, whilst the eroticization of the model is made abundantly clear in the regular inclusion of fashion editorial for perfume 'Heaven Scent' (centre left Figure 4). In this instance, the erotic takes precedence. As Simpson observes, it is perfume/aftershave adverts in the mainstream media that have produced the most overt and narcissistic objectification of the naked male torso. But where homoeroticized perfume adverts in the mainstream produce a troublingly queer ambivalence in which the homoerotic desire for the male body must be to some extent disavowed (Simpson, 1994), their presence as editorial in *Attitude* produces the erotic as the dominant meaning: an unproblematic source of pleasure.

We can no longer simply talk about preferred and alternative meanings when the makers of mainstream aftershave adverts clearly know they are producing polysemic and queer imagery – the problem becomes one of relationships *between* meanings in which the viewer's decoding activities may operate from a variety of positions each of which utilizes a different set of competencies that may be addressed by the text.

Figure 5 *Eroticizing the Image*. Photograph: Simon Pattle.

It is hard to imagine a naked perfume promotion in *Diva*, although the American magazine *Girlfriends* regularly contains a centrefold and a variety of overtly eroticized images. But *Girlfriends* is also more adventurous in its fashion coverage (Figure 5) with spreads that seem to me to be more eroticized than those in *Diva*.

This greater ease, or willingness to play, with fashion may be because of the different attitudes to consumption in American feminism, where feminists have been more likely to organize campaigns around women's power as consumers than in the UK. Or it may simply be that *Diva* is not aiming for the erotic and *Girlfriends*, which features much pro-sex content and is associated with the *On our backs* crowd, is. But it is also to do with the more developed narratives of the *Girlfriends'* spreads. This investment in narrative produces similar possibilities for visual pleasure as those Katrina and I detected in mainstream magazines. The range of lesbian positionalities signified within each narrative affords a variety of points of access, identification and objectification.

In some magazines, fashion replaces or has a similar status to erotica, which was previously the place where style and visual transgression were housed. What, one might wonder, is the relationship between visuals in

Girlfriend that are coded as fashion, those identified as erotic and others that are labelled as 'portfolio' (artists' photographs which are also style-driven in content)?

The ambivalence that seems to be possible in *Attitude* but not in *Diva* may also be linked to the ownership of the look at the point of production: where *Diva* uses only lesbian photographers, *Attitude* and *Girlfriends* feature photographers of both genders and unspecified sexual orientation. Kobena Mercer, in his analysis of the homosexual pleasures available to him in Mapplethorpe's difficult and ambiguous images of black men, argues that it matters very much who is looking (Mercer, 1994). He insists that it is Mapplethorpe's insertion of himself into the subcultural scene he represents (via the self-portraits) that allows him to construct himself and hence the viewer as both owner and object of the homoerotic gaze, leading to a 'participatory observation' and 'ironic ethnography' (Mercer, 1994: 195). But in *Attitude* we do not know if the photographer is gay, although they are certainly gay-literate. In *Diva* we do know that the photograph's point of origin is female and can assume from the politics of the magazine that this is lesbian. In *Girlfriends* we know that sometimes the photographer is male. But here, another set of subcultural competencies associated with a lesbian sadomasochism and a pro-sex discourse can intervene to assert a cross-gender, cross-sexuality community of interest that protects a male-produced image from charges of invalidity. In terms of the specific subcultural competencies that are mobilized by *Girlfriends* (its adverts, editorial and features) the inclusion of male photographers' erotic lesbian images becomes an assertion of a lesbian identity that transgresses a subcultural orthodoxy coded variously as vanilla, lesbian and feminist.

If fashion is an arena noted for the transience and instability of its meaning and values, what is its relationship to a field of cultural production driven in part by a desire for certainty (there must be a mass of subjects who identify as lesbian or gay in order to provide a market for the product) where some readers welcome ambivalence in the dominant but are inclined to be anxious about it when encountered in the subcultural? Mercer argues that ambivalence signals the presence of an ideological struggle over meaning. In relation to dominant definitions, this has the potential to be politically progressive: for him, the indecipherability of Mapplethorpe's pictures of black men reveals the ambivalence of the racial fetishization (in which black men are both feared and adored) against which stereotype the very foundations of whiteness as an identity rest. But, in the case of lesbian and gay lifestyle magazines, the destabilization produced by the ambivalent fashion image is not of a dominant norm, but of a subcultural identity that often sees itself as already counter-hegemonic. So what does the

FEMINIST REVIEW NO 55, SPRING 1997

recognition of ambivalence give us in this instance? Well, it suggests that lesbian and gay modes of reading are varied and operate differently in different contexts. But it also suggests that this contingency does not just depend on the object consumed but also on the stability of the consumer's sense of self. Without the surety of a dominant heterosexual stereotype to transgress, lesbianism becomes worryingly hard to detect.

Conclusion: dress, recognizability and transgression

It seems that in the case of fashion spreads lesbian visual pleasure disappears when it is with the grain. Fashion, perhaps, has an easier potential to provide pleasure for gay men, for whom an interest in fashion is often still coded as transgressive, than for lesbians, many of whom experienced fashion as a route to heterosexual conformity. Of course, other forms of lesbian culture, such as film and literature, do manage to produce lesbian pleasures with the grain. So what is specific about fashion? If it is the exercise of a subcultural competency in the act of interpretation that produces pleasure, rather than only the image itself, then maybe fashion with all its potential for visual splendour also needs to evoke narrative? It may be the potential to construct fantasy through narrativized readings that ensures the eroticized lesbian pleasures in the consumption of fashion imagery. Certainly, some narratives can more easily be made to bear same-sex investments than others, but it is probably the absence of narrative in many *Diva* spreads that accounts for their lukewarm reception. Of course, effectively constructing the sort of rich and evocative narrative structures that are so pleasurable in mainstream fashion spreads also tends to cost money, so access to higher production values as well as editorial choice would have an impact here. But it does seem that the more suggestive a spread was, the more my totally unrepresentative group of viewers liked them. But an investment in narrative need not necessarily have to be against the grain, although the reception of gay magazines suggests that lesbian and gay consumers do prefer to read oppositionally. This may be a learned habit, shared with other groups marginalized from or 'misrepresented' in dominant forms of culture (hooks, 1992), but it does not explain why many heterosexuals, who might be seen as not very marginal, also who prefer the connoted to the denoted. If there is a specifically subcultural investment in oppositional reading practices, how does this transfer to artifacts with subcultural conditions of production?

In this light, the mixed response to the introduction of fashion into new lesbian and gay lifestyle magazines needs to be situated in relation to other visuals in gay-produced culture, to dominant images of lesbians and gays and to changing dominant images of femininity and masculinity, as well as to the increasingly problematic relationship of style to identity for lesbian subcultures. When identity can no longer be decoded from appearance, fashion is both a newly available playground and a danger zone of irrecognizability.

Notes

Reina Lewis teaches in the Department of Cultural Studies at the University of East London. She is author of *Gendering Orientalism: Race, Femininity and Representation* (1996, London: Routledge) and co-editor with Peter Horne of *Outlooks: Lesbian and Gay Sexualities and Visual Cultures* (1996, London: Routledge).

I would like to thank Peter Horne and Caroline Evans for their comments on an earlier version of this piece. I am grateful to Frances Williams, Robert Pardoe and Paula Graham for sharing their supply of magazines with me.

1 Murray Healy, conference presentation at Postmodern Times, City University, July 1995.

References

CLARK, Danae (1993) 'Commodity lesbianism' in **Abelove, Barale** and **Halperin**, editors *The Lesbian and Gay Studies Reader* London: Routledge.

EVANS, Caroline and THORNTON, Minna (1989) *Women and Fashion: A New Look* London: Quartet.

—— and **GAMMAN, Lorraine** (1995) 'The gaze revisited, or reviewing queer viewing' in **Burston** and **Richardson**, editors *A Queer Romance: Lesbians, Gay Men and Popular Culture* London: Routledge.

FUSS, Diane (1992) 'Fashion and the homospectatorial look' *Critical Inquiry* Vol. 18, Summer: 713–37.

hooks, bell (1992) *Black Looks: Race and Representation* London: Turnaround.

LEWIS, Reina and ROLLEY, Katrina (1996) '(A)dressing the dyke: lesbian looks and lesbians looking' in **Horne** and **Lewis**, editors *Outlooks: Lesbian and Gay Sexualities and Visual Culture* London: Routledge.

MERCER, Kobena (1994) *Welcome to the Jungle: New Positions in Black Cultural Studies* London: Routledge.

MORT, Frank (1996) *Cultures of Consumption: Masculinities and Social Space in Late Twentieth-Century Britain* London: Routledge.

O'SULLIVAN, Sue (1994) 'Girls who kiss girls and who cares?' in **Hamer** and **Budge**, editors *The Good, the Bad and the Gorgeous: Popular Culture's Romance with Lesbianism* London: Pandora.

SIMPSON, Mark (1994) *Male Impersonators* London: Cassell.

WALKER, Lisa M. (1993) 'How to recognize a lesbian: the cultural politics of looking like what you are' *Signs: Journal of Women in Culture and Society* Vol. 18, No. 4.

Gender, 'Race', Ethnicity in Art Practice in Post-Apartheid South Africa:

Annie E. Coombes and Penny Siopis in Conversation*

Annie E. Coombes

FEMINIST REVIEW NO 55, SPRING 1997, pp. 110–29

Abstract

Siopis has always engaged in a critical and controversial way with the concepts of 'race' and 'ethnicity' in South Africa. For politically sensitive artists whose work has involved confronting the injustices of apartheid, the current post-apartheid situation has forced a reassessment of their practice and the terms on which they might engage with the fundamental changes which are now affecting all of South African society. Where mythologies of race and ethnicity have been strategically foregrounded in the art of any engaged artist, to the exclusion of many other concerns, the demise of apartheid offers the possibility of exploring other dimensions of lived experience in South Africa. For feminists, this is potentially a very positive moment when questions of gender – so long subordinated to the structural issue of 'race' under apartheid – can now be explored. Penny Siopis' work has long been concerned with the lived and historical relations between black and white women in South Africa. The discussion focuses on the ambivalent and dependent relationships formed between white middle-class women and black domestic labour during apartheid. Siopis' work engages with how the appropriation of black women's time, lives, labour and bodies has shaped her 'own' history.

Keywords

apartheid; South Africa; feminist art practice; appropriation; Saartjie Baartman; consumption; culture; Penny Siopis; Annie Coombes

Annie Coombes: It seems to me that one of the primary concerns in your work is a very difficult, thorny issue – the issue of subjectivity and subjection as articulated through a set of domestic relations within the home, relations in which 'race' figures predominantly. The problem of different subjectivities surfaces very specifically in the works which deal with what you importantly signal as the ambivalent relationship between a white childhood's dependency on a black nanny, where nannies were part of the domestic sphere. For me these works raise the issue of how innocence and power are reflected and enacted by and through the process of racialization in that relationship. There are two things I want to tease out here. So the first question concerns the idea of subjectivity in your work, and the links you're attempting to make in a number of the pieces, between the racialization of the working-class black women and the negation of her subjectivity through that process. Perhaps your *Tula-Tula* series embodies these ideas most clearly (Figure 1). But your work also suggests that at some level there is a *shared* history of pathologizing sexuality to which both black and white women have been subjected in South Africa. How do you make a clear distinction between the kind of pathologization through racialization on the one hand, and on the other, the history of how white women's sexuality has also been contained and confined through the oppressive structures of apartheid?

Penny Siopis: It is a distinction that I found difficult to untangle. Patriarchal oppression occurs in both, but the mediating factors are complex and differentiated. I wouldn't say there is an equivalence of a shared relationship but I think there's something to be said for both which is produced around gender. I think it's a bit like the problem of actually talking about women in any general way. I think one has to first make a kind of general point that there is something, if you like, in common, but not necessarily equivalent, and certainly not equivalent in this situation, because obviously the pathologizing of gender is one thing, but then there's another thing which makes an issue of race, which is a kind of double subjection for black women.

AC: You see I think that this is also further complicated, particularly in the South African context. In your work there seems to be a historical slippage between the representation of the control and pathologizing of white women and their sexuality, which is specifically located in the nineteenth century, and the divide between white and black experience which continues today. In other words one can be very clearly located and specifically seen as something which is of the past (although the ramifications continue in all sorts of ways), but the other has a very clear presence in the way in which lived relations are played out, especially in South Africa, between black and white women and also in terms generally of black women's experience here. So I think it's a really sensitive issue and it's very difficult to negotiate in a way that doesn't reduce women to an essentialist category. Do you think that there is a danger that that historical slippage then creates another kind of slippage where the differences between the power relations, between white women and black women are erased?

PS: I think in a way this is almost impossible to answer. What I have tried to do is rather open up the question. The question of difference you point to

Figure 1 Penny Siopis, *Tula-Tula 1*, 1993–4, photocopy, photograph, steel wool, found object (Victorian frame), oil on board, 111 x 67cm.

is not stable. I consciously exhibited just the traces of these women, the outward signs of women who worked as nannies in white households, for example. Everyone in South Africa knows that the uniforms in *Maids* are the

Figure 2 Penny Siopis, *Foreign Affairs (Arutma)*, 1994, photocopies, found objects, oil on board, 100.5 x 246cm.

uniforms of black maids. I specifically wanted them exhibited in close proximity to *Foreign Affairs* (Figure 2). *Foreign Affairs* is a work using images of medieval restraints and scolds' bridles together with an image of Saartjie Baartman. Her face is centred on a mirror. When you look into it, it is as if you are held there by her. The images of the scolds' bridles are interspersed with texts from the *Weekly Mail* newspaper published during the State of Emergency.

AC: During that period whole paragraphs and sentences in various newspapers were inked out by the censor?

PS: Not exactly. The *Weekly Mail* chose the device of blackening out text or leaving white spaces to signal the work of suppression of information. I wanted to suggest a relationship between contemporary censorship and ideas about having the right to speak – having or not having a voice. The medieval masks are also about speaking, or not being able to speak. If women spoke too much they were punished and things put on their faces, restraints on their tongues. This brings me back to the issue of subjectivity – subjectivity in terms of how my subjectivity would be produced or changed, having had the experience of being brought up or nannied by a black woman, and how hers might be altered. So in a way that whole relationship between class, race, subjectivity and the idea of gender was for me an enquiry into all those things and the ideas that almost can't be spoken. I wanted to try to face it, not erase it or avoid it. The last would have been simpler and easier, but not viable for me.

AC: The issue of subjectivity and power relations particularly between the white child and the black nanny in South Africa is especially complex.

PC: Yes, and that's why it's interesting to deal with. In some ways the black nanny may seem to have the power if you like, when she's bringing up the small white child. But she's always disadvantaged, even when she has that little baby, who she loves like her own child and who loves her, in a sense, like a mother. Then that relationship changes as the boy becomes an adolescent and older. What interests me is what happens in that experience. My interest here was probably stimulated, provoked or sharpened by the birth of my own child.

AC: So one of the aims of your work is to signal the difficult ambiguities of that relationship – the loss in a sense, on both sides as well as the complex power relationship. In other words you want to make explicit that forbidden longing which is later denied in adulthood, by the white male child?

PS: Yes, amongst other things. There's trauma involved like the trauma involved when a child loses his mother. There's trauma for the mother, and if one tries to read this psychoanalytically, the child has to have trauma to have a voice. The mother in effect loses her voice. In South Africa for white women this is not necessarily the case, but for black women that actually is the case in reality, so what I tried to do in *Tula-Tula* (Figure 1) is make a physical and material representation of the loss of that voice which actually doesn't happen to white women. This is a 'difference' of the kind you mentioned earlier. White women actually have power. I wouldn't say they have power in quite the same way as white men. They don't. But they have or have had, for instance, more power than black men.

AC: And that power actually relies on a relationship with black women based on their subjection. So it's a relationship of both dependence and subjection.

PS: Yes, and what I'm trying to do is draw attention to the fact that there are some similarities possible through gender emanating from patriarchal oppression and there are some connections that can be made across class and race. But there are, of course, differences too, perhaps absolute, that remain separated no matter what you think.

AC: One of the series which plays on that ambivalent relationship of dependence, subjection and shared identifications is *Royal Vermont: Hand Painted (Zulu Maiden)* and *Royal Vermont: Hand painted (Ndebele Girl)*. The piece consists of two plates, one with an adolescent Zulu girl and the other depicting a young Ndebele girl framed on different grounds. The choice of the term 'maiden' is very specific, it seems to me, since it signals an adolescent girl entering into puberty. In *Royal Vermont: Hand Painted (Zulu Maiden)* the ground is composed of white plastic ponytail clips which might in some ways seem more appropriate as a sign of white adolescent girlhood. So in these works you seem to be signalling a kind of shared rite of passage to adult womanhood which *all* girls go through in different ways. They *all* have certain things in common; the accoutrements of adolescence and a preoccupation with body decoration. You seem to be suggesting that there's a way in which young white girls and also the 'Zulu maiden' or the 'Ndebele maiden' could be seen as having some kind of shared experience. These works also signal the domestic sphere through the use of objects which are particularly coded for a South African viewer. The ground of one piece, for example, is made up of what we would call in Britain 'brillo pads', scourers whose brand name in South Africa is 'Goldilocks'. Such objects are very familiar in the context of black women's domestic labour. So, similar to *Glass and Race, Pale* and *Glass and Race, Dark* (Figure 3) which suggested a connection between the pathologization and racialization of black and white women, there's a different kind of link between black and white women's experience being suggested here also?

PS: You could put that kind of reading onto it, although for me the pony-tail clips are more importantly markers of absence and the scourers are intended as a racial pun in the wider sense. The experience of having a black nanny would have meant more to my brothers or to men and to my white male child. What's difficult is that the trauma that the white male suffers also in some measure afflicts the black woman because she loses, not only her voice, but her authority – little as it was – in relation to white women. She had something with this child. Then she loses the child. The child quite literally goes away to school and she is structured into a different relationship with it which involves rejection. That child becomes a person who calls her by a name that is not her name, that orders her around. He might even use her body sexually, and he becomes the boss, the master. The loss that she suffers is all the greater because she has experienced a genuine affection both from and for the child who has now withdrawn from her. And he must suffer some loss in relation to that black woman. And I suppose what I'm trying to work through is the nature of that loss, such trauma which occurred in the apartheid years – things that can't be spoken. I'm completely fascinated by this incredibly powerful constellation of relations and feelings as something that is just so much part of this society and cries for representation.

AC: Do you think you've actually been able to represent in some way that psychic dimension of loss to both parties that you were talking about?

PS: There is an asymmetry here. I cannot and do not claim to do justice to 'both' parties. I've tried to put objects which speak, if you like, socially and psychoanalytically. These objects are resonant, suggestive.

AC: The three works which make up the *Tula-Tula* series, perhaps more than any other, try and resolve in a representational form the absent

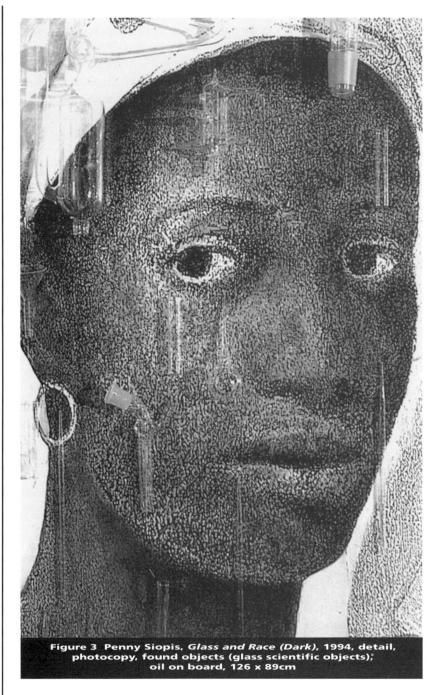

Figure 3 Penny Siopis, *Glass and Race (Dark)*, 1994, detail, photocopy, found objects (glass scientific objects), oil on board, 126 x 89cm

psychic dimension of that loss. You've deliberately used the image of your brother as a child as a way of bringing in a personal dimension.

PS: I've used a blown-up negative from a photo of my brother with his nanny. The image itself is very suggestive in terms of the mother/child relationship. The nanny is sitting down with him on her lap and his hand is on hers. There are lots of details which would signify to a South African viewer – the child's little hat, his sandals – things typical of a white little boy child. I've tried to work up the negative spaces of the photocopy, particularly around her face and his face. Because it is a photographic negative, she's in fact white, if you like, colourwise, and he's black, but his eyes are white. I've tried to invert value-laden colour. His eyes are in some ways absent or blank because in the original photograph they would have been black. Thinking psychoanalytically about vision and power the child's 'blank' eyes and the nanny's gaze become crucial details. She looks down at him and he looks out at the viewer. I've also deliberately and painstakingly built up her face materially with paint because I wanted to produce a strong point of identification. The act of painting, the physical presence of working up the surface tends to create an affective relationship which may help shift the term away from harsh binaries of self and other. Then there's the Victorian frame which is incorporated into the image, framing a 'field' of steel wool (like flattened brillo pads) and a photograph. The photograph shows part of an inscription of a monument in Pretoria. The monument was erected in the 1980s in honour of the 'victims of terrorism'. Obviously the victims were supposed to be white and terrorists assumed to be black. So I've used the inscription, 'terrorisme', an Afrikaans word, and juxtaposed it with the image. The word points to an actual historic monument in South Africa and has arisen from an identifiable historical period of oppression. In a sense it signals the idea of the split identities of black women as both 'comfort' and 'threat', as perceived by white people under apartheid. Black women were obviously seen as the people who would look after their children, love their children. But at the same time they're seen as the 'enemy'.

AC: And, of course, what their relationship with the white child effectively did was remove from black women the opportunity to care for their own children or indeed, in some cases, to even produce their own children. So this was yet another form of containment under apartheid.

PS: Yes, and another thing which interests me is that the nanny's role of surrogate mother also made her a threatening figure and the target of many myths during the years of the 'swart gevaar' or 'black peril'. During this time there were always stories going around that if, for instance there was going to be a black take-over that one of the most terrifying places would be in the domestic space because that was where black women had power and opportunity. And I experienced an anxiety about that so-called split subject – my beloved nanny – when I was little. That in the end makes the subjectivity of black women really complex and virtually impossible to represent for me, other than through lots of fractured, different stories and different images and different ways.

AC: The thing which interests me about the *Tula-Tula* series is that here the ambivalences are contained within a single series and repeated in different ways. The fact that you gave it the name of a famous Zulu lullaby – tula-tula – is also significant. Again it's about a potentially 'shared' experience between black and white. Paradoxically the white child recognizes and is soothed by the lullaby which also nurses and comforts the black child. At the same time the pose in the snapshot is resonant of Christian religious iconography and consequently the viewer becomes conscious of an uncomfortable juxtaposition between violence ('terrorisme') and the nurturing sacrifices one might associate with the Madonna figure.

PS: 'Tula' is also a command to 'keep quiet' or 'become quiet'. If one thinks of the sign of 'tula-tula' you hear the voice of a black woman and that's a kind of nourishment.

AC: You mentioned the difficulties in dealing with subjectivity. One of the big questions this raises is whether or not it's possible or even desirable to try and represent, or signal, another kind of subjectivity for black women in South Africa, especially as a white woman. Related to this issue is the fact that many of the representations of black women in your work are representations of subjection. Do you think there could be a charge levelled at you in the sense that the images and the sign of black women in your work is constantly one of subjection, and that the voices and experiences of resistance and agency for example, are not actually present except in signalling the ambivalent relationship between the white child and the nanny?

I ask because I've been very aware having just spent a few months in South Africa of the incredible ways in which *any* women who were committed to challenging the regime and involved in the struggle, but in particular black women, have been almost erased from representations of the history of the Liberation. You rarely see acknowledgement of the repercussions for women, of the 'Bantu' system or apartheid's policy of 'separate development' which forced the women to carry on an independent life with very few resources, separated from their husbands, where they continued the struggle on the domestic front. I find it disturbing that there's so little acknowledgement in the official representations of the struggle here of the activity of women. Even the famous domestic workers' march in Pretoria in the 1950s is never chosen as one of the constantly repeated iconic images of the struggle. On the domestic front and in the homelands during apartheid, women were absolutely central. You could even say that black women made the whole thing possible. There seems to be a kind of amnesia about women's struggles and women's voices. It is a depressingly predictable absence. It may seem a bit crude, but I wondered if you had considered this in terms of the kinds of images of women that you're using in your work?

PS: I think this is a really interesting question. I have never felt confident about representing black women's resistance and would feel uncomfortable with my work being read like that. I am interested in relationships, not speaking *for* people. I am speaking for myself. Other people are involved of course and this has implications concerning race, class, gender. But what I did do in the earlier works, in, for example, the history paintings, is to place the presence of black women, as historical protagonists, in the frame, in the picture, on the historical stage. Yet even here there is an ambivalence which interests me. In later works it's been different because I shifted focus into other aspects of power relations. The way representation of the struggle and in particular representations of women in the struggle has in fact now been taken up by people in power, by the ANC, for example, has changed things a little. There have been programmes on television and in the electronic media about women in the struggle. But these representations could be seen as problematic because they legitimatize a patriarchal discourse to look as if there is an acknowledgement of women's role in the Liberation struggle. In this sense it may be something of an empty gesture, especially if one takes into account that the focus of these programmes is often on women as the power *behind* the struggle. Before we had the transitional government, for example, there was a clause that stated that each region of the country had to have delegates of both sexes, so there were women around, but those women didn't speak much, they weren't significantly empowered. But for all this, my interest in the exhibition of my work 'Private Views' in September 1994 was not about reflecting on this kind of question. I wanted to explore more the internal complexities of my own experience of being racialized.

AC: So in a sense, 'Private Views' was a very personal exhibition exploring your own subjectivity?

PS: Yes. The change of government and the slow changes in power relations has given many artists and certainly me the chance to be able to explore these things and I think that's actually very productive. The psychic dynamics of what's been going on have not been sufficiently dealt with because there's been little space to do this in culture. It's tended to be about positioning, about contestation, about opposition – these are the issues and this is how you relate to them.

AC: And did you also feel obliged, strategically, to make that position explicit so that it was less ambiguous to the viewers?

PS: I think that the confusions or ambivalences that are part of my work seem more viable because now there is the time for reflection. It's also part of trying to understand the larger questions, why there's been racism in this country and how to come to terms with being implicated in that history of racism as a white woman.

AC: I would like to turn now to one of the figures that has consistently appeared in your work over the years: the image of Saartjie Baartman. The work of scholars like Sander Gilman and Bernth Lindfors have been important in bringing her complicated history to light – the way she was displayed as a freak spectacle for the delectation of European audiences in the nineteenth century and the European fascination with her buttocks, particularly the steatopygia and also her genitals. It was a fascination which resulted in the final invasion of her body under the French scientist Cuvier's scrutiny, when he dissected her genitals and then published his findings as an illustrated document. She's clearly an iconic figure for you and provides a thread which runs through all your work. For me it's a very interesting thread because her case obviously highlights very clearly the historical relationship between science, pathology and the masquerade of scientific objectivity, particularly in the development of racism. It also highlights the way in which women's sexuality, and black women's sexuality in particular, was pathologized and spectacularized.

You've also talked about the importance of the work of Julia Kristeva for you and it seemed to me the way in which you were engaging with the figure of Saartjie Baartman was as the sign of the 'abject', in the sense of abjection that Kristeva discusses. For example, for Europeans, Baartman was evidently an object of both disgust and desire through their scopophilic obsession with her genitals. Representations of her are constantly inscribed within this notion of the 'abject' and within a pathologizing discourse. These are also very negative images of a black woman because she has no voice, has never in fact been given a voice, despite the wealth of scholarship which has centred around her case. The focus has been very much on different aspects of that history and on the way in which European representations of her and the circulation of her images reproduced certain obsessions with black women's sex. Could you say something about the way her representation functions for you? In what ways is she iconic and how can you use Kristeva's concept of the 'abject' productively? How might you be using the historic figure of Baartman to say something about the relationship between the representation of black and white women's sexuality in South Africa?

PS: I think what interests me is how, as you said, she's both an object of fascination and disgust. She's an emblem for me, she's a story. She is also a real person which is a sign for the way racism functions in some ways, even now, even though she's a historical figure, how fetishism works. Its often said that the site of difference in relation to women is the genitals and that with race the site of that difference is say colour, skin colour. So for me Baartman's story and representations of her raises huge issues in this country around the conjunction of gender and race, sexuality and race and there are many reasons why I suppose I have been affected by her story. As a sign she seems to do that for many people. Yet her story, because it's quite singular and what happened to her is not a theory, not a distant thing, even though she's a long-gone historical figure – has actually been incredibly productive in raising critical issues around the relationship between gender and race in South Africa. So I suppose that's how she's functioned in the public domain, and although it's very sensitive material to use, there is something very important about engaging with this material.

AC: You've been consistently concerned to explore the relationship between black women and white women's sexuality. But how does your use of historical representations of Baartman impact on the kinds of links you want to make in relation to the way in which white women's sexuality has also been historically inscribed within a particular kind of pathologizing discourse?

PS: White women are often absent from Baartman's story. I've tried to address this. In *Dora and the Other Woman* I've looked at Saartjie Baartman in relation to Freud's Dora and I have been quite explicit about the relationship here. Dora's sexuality was fragmented, taken away from her, in a sense by Freud. She was made an object. While her genitals weren't literally put into a bottle and preserved like Saartjie Baartman, she too was actually objectified and turned into a spectacle. In that work I copied quite literally and painstakingly nineteenth-century French and British caricatures of people looking at Saartjie Baartman. The idea of looking and the idea of objectification was the connecting theme in both those women's stories. But clearly even within that scenario power relations are played out 'differently'. That is why I used caricatures. They were obviously representations, I was simply re-representing them. So on this occasion I actually made a direct connection between the way white women's sexuality was pathologized in psychoanalysis, most of all through Freud, and the image of Saartjie Baartman. But more recently I started using the cast of Saartjie's face because it is in fact the nearest to a trace of her we have. It's like an indexical sign. It's as close as one could get, I suppose, but it's still a mediation, it's a cast. When I've used Baartman's image, I've always marked it as a mediation even in the subtlest of senses. This has involved including the odd contingent effects of the contexts which framed her – the packing crates, the protective cushions, etc.

Figure 4 Penny Siopis, *Exhibit Ex-Africa*, 1990, found object, collage, screenprint, oil paint, 126.2 × 124.5 cms. Johannesburg Art Gallery.

AC: So, for instance, in some of the other works, for example *Exhibit Ex-Africa*, you don't include a representation of the cast of Baartman's genitals but a 'real' piece of cloth, a Victorian 'apron', as a way of suggesting the cloth which was wrapped around the cast of her body parts in the storeroom of the Musée de L'Homme in Paris where you saw them (Figure 4)?

PS: Yes. But the apron also obviously refers to the 'tablier' – a term used to refer to the shape of her genitals.

AC: I've seen the photographs which you took of the plaster casts of Saartjie Baartman at the Musée de L'Homme and the way in which she's literally packaged and crated in the storeroom of the museum. And I've also seen those horrific casts of different African women's genitals, totally disembodied with anus and vagina wrapped in cloth, in a kind of fetishistic embrace with the cloth opening out onto the plaster casts of truncated genital areas. These are very disturbing images.

PS: Yes, they are disturbing images, but what is interesting is that the cloth seems to function as a cover for the break, the edge of the cast where the leg would normally appear. I haven't ever, and I probably never will, use the images of the genitals, but I'm interested in the idea that there was some kind of need to cover a break but leave the genitals truncated, sectioned and exposed. The impulse seems to have been to cover the sign of the objectification – of the object. It seems to be a displacement of a most extraordinary kind. It's as if they don't really want to show what's really happened, namely the cutting up of this person's body. So they disguise the cut.

AC: In relation to the act of viewing what this seems to do is suspend or extend the 'fantasy'. It suspends disbelief. In other words, by covering the suture it also enables a kind of voyeuristic fantasy to continue.

PS: It doesn't reveal the terms of its violent construction and that's what's really interesting.

AC: In *Exhibit Ex-Africa*, for example, you've shown the cloth (the 'tablier') with, as it were, an absent centre. For those of us who have seen those photos of the casts at the Musée de L'Homme this is a very poignant image. But a lot of your work deals with the question of subjectivity (your own in particular), and sometimes this involves using symbolic items that are only really accessible to you. Perhaps the image of the cloth wrapped around its absent centre is one of these. I've seen the photographs that you took surreptitiously at the Musée de L'Homme. I know the absent centre that they disclose, but most viewers of *Exhibit Ex-Africa* won't. So there are different levels of meaning in your work, as with many artists. There are always spaces which are not necessarily accessible and can only be appreciated through a different kind of interrogation of the work on a very personal level. And then there are other figures which are so iconic that there is no mistaking aspects of their significance, like the figure of Saartjie Baartman. Do you see the more obscure references as a problem in work which purports to be so centrally concerned with larger political issues?

PS: I think things sometimes function metonymically. There's a sense if you look at that cloth, even if you don't know what it is, you would soon realize that it is covering something up, so to speak. This could be seen then as something 'missing'. The cloth then, placed in close proximity as it is to the more obviously identifiable images of Saartjie Baartman, would be read through the context that her images produce. This kind of ambiguous lack is really important to me. I think it makes the viewer active in projecting meaning. I would not want my work to be seen simply as didactically political, so I would not see this degree of ambiguity as a problem in relation to the apparent political positioning of my practice. What I found

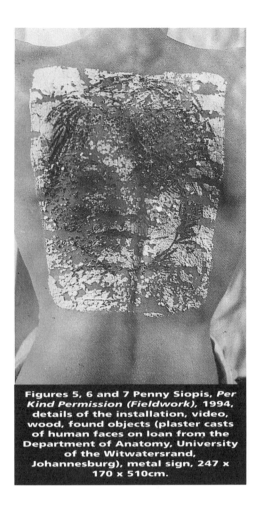

Figures 5, 6 and 7 Penny Siopis, *Per Kind Permission (Fieldwork),* **1994, details of the installation, video, wood, found objects (plaster casts of human faces on loan from the Department of Anatomy, University of the Witwatersrand, Johannesburg), metal sign, 247 x 170 x 510cm.**

interesting is when I took those photographs I felt very voyeuristic, horrified and shocked all at once. I also felt that I *should* see these things. It was an odd sort of defiance. I needed to see them but I was horrified nonetheless. I photographed them and I've had the photographs for years.

AC: Those casts in the Musée de L'Homme are powerfully horrifying objects. Much of your own work has dealt with the idea of the cast, the imprint of the body's traces. For example in the video *Per Kind Permission: Fieldwork* (Figures 5, 6, 7) you've used the repetitive and painful act of plastering, spraying and scraping your own back as a reference to the process of casting in the nineteenth and early twentieth centuries. In the video, the violence that's enacted on your own body as part of this activity is suggestive of the physical pain and discomfort which was inevitably part of the process of casting bodies either for ethnographic displays or for anatomical museums in the past.

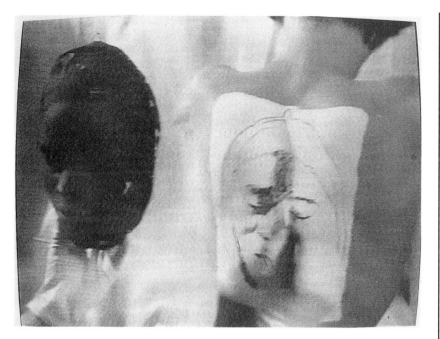

PS: And in those days the technology of casting was actually very primitive. Your face would cave in, you'd get sores under your eyes, you'd bruise and get straws up your nose for breathing. Just actually taking the cast was an extremely uncomfortable and painful business.

AC: A lot of people in South Africa recently have become more aware of the historical use of casting and the kind of intrusion that it represents, especially in ethnographic museums. In the South Africa Museum, in Cape Town, rather than destroy the evidence of this history, curators have retained the notorious ethnographic diorama display of the Khoi-San people. As a strategy for unmasking the racist assumptions of these early dioramas, Patricia Davison and her colleagues have erected another display beside it, which actually narrates the history of how those casts were taken from named individuals while they were alive, and describes the very intrusive techniques employed. It's a very controversial diorama because of the evolutionist assumptions about the Khoi-San and it's very well known here in South Africa. So there's a way in which some of your work is particularly poignant in the South African context. For example, in this case, because of the notoriety of the Cape Town display and the violence that it represented to different communities.

AC: If Saartjie Baartman's story could be seen as paradigmatic of a western scopic impulse do you think it is also necessary to address what Gayatri Chakravorty Spivak has spoken of as the need for a 'simultaneous other focus'? In other words do you think it is important to engage in the 'other' side of this colonizing gaze or is this impossible without doing epistemic violence?

PS: Certainly I have given much thought to this. I am interested in the question of epistemic violence and have struggled to find a way to work through this issue in making art. I think for me art is exactly the place to do this. As an overdetermined practice I feel art offers a space to search and tease things out a little. What is very important for me is that I do whatever I do within the context of a relationship in which I am obviously and often visibly implicated.

AC: Something you've also spoken about is your concern to make 'whiteness' 'visible' in your work and to address the way in which it has become a transparent, naturalized category.

PS: I've been nervous about exploring 'whiteness' and I think I was even nervous when I worked with the idea of making an issue of an apparently invisible whiteness, facing 'race', which meant whiteness as well as blackness. But I think that it is always a difficult thing to start talking about whiteness if you are white, especially in South Africa at the moment, when there are other kinds of discourses, or shall I say popular myths around whiteness, which are actually very reactionary. My interest in whiteness as a concept could be confused with the misconception of whiteness as 'ethnicity'.

AC: Do you mean the whole issue of acknowledging white ethnicities as well as black, as part of a supposedly 'progressive' agenda, but one which might wrongly suggest an immediate equivalence of power – a kind of power sharing?

PS: Exactly, and this is not the case even under the new democracy. Why I want to produce these images here is specifically in relation to the media and the kinds of myths that are being produced and the way in which some are trying to assert whiteness as a positive thing now, in the best sense, as 'white' was also positive under apartheid of course. To some degree, I can understand this. But I think it can, once again, erase, suppress or distort lived relations in this country.

AC: I think in South Africa in particular, the whole issue of how to make visible that absent centre, the idea of whiteness, is very very difficult especially if you deal with it as a category of ethnicity because it can so easily be confused with the apartheid rhetoric of 'separate but equal development' that depended on a particular concept of 'ethnicity'. That whole notion of ethnicity here, because it's been part of the political project and ideology of apartheid, makes it so much more difficult to unpack the idea of white ethnicities and how these have been constructed, without reproducing the worst aspects of that ideology.

PS: Strictly speaking, white ethnicity does not exist. There is Afrikaner ethnicity, for example, in which race (as in white) is of fundamental importance. But the whole issue is very complex. That is why I have been held back in many ways. I suppose I couldn't find the forms for dealing with 'whiteness' without falling into that trap.

AC: Is there a kind of a crisis in terms of areas of representation for people working as visual artists here? Is there a way in which a whole body, a whole iconography, a whole way of framing one's work is now no longer viable? For example, the issue of gender can be raised in a way that wasn't something that many artists felt they could prioritize previously if they were committed to the struggle against apartheid. All those 'grey' areas were politically and strategically not useful things to focus on at that time. So, it seems that now, there's both a crisis and a new freedom for artists. The way some critics are now responding to your own work is perhaps symptomatic of this shift – and it signals a potentially new problem. Are you concerned with the way artists are, in some quarters, now being encouraged to see aesthetics and politics as necessarily autonomous realms, partly as a respite after the more explicitly 'political' work during apartheid? Is there a danger that work like yours, which engages with the subjective and the private might easily be read as comfortably a-political in this context?

PS: In a way. And it makes my practice very problematic because if I do want to explore the political dimension of sexuality and the realm of privacy it does not mean that I am giving up the political at all. Just because one's not literally painting images of the liberation struggle does not mean that you are not political, or that you don't have a political positioning personally apart from the context of the work.

AC: Are you anxious that your work is now going to be recuperated into a much less politicized set of discourses around which sexuality is seen as a way of escaping an engagement with some of the more difficult issues post-apartheid?

PS: This is always a risk. It always was. In fact strongly 'political work' was appropriated itself in the past. I think that we're going to see a lot of such displacement in the public realm. What's already happening in the work around sexuality that's been done, especially with the younger generation of women artists, is that they've tended to be interested in what they call 'post-feminism' and not politics – as if somehow the issue of gender is now neutral, neither here nor there, or more about sexual preference and pleasure. They don't even seem to acknowledge that pleasure has a political dimension.

AC: The 'post-feminism' agenda is something which is also common to Europe and North America. But what's interesting is that I think here in South Africa, it's framed in a very particular way. A lot of women that weren't engaged in the struggle and who maybe even supported apartheid through apathy and through indifference are probably only too relieved to agree with this agenda, since it effectively lets everyone off the hook. And now there's a furious celebration of pleasure, but an uncritical pleasure, devoid of a recognition of the way in which pleasure itself is socially and also politically constituted. It's almost an evacuation of the 'political' all together, partly out of guilt, perhaps, as a result of collusion in this history of criminal indifference. There seems to be a desire on the part of some artists also to absolutely erase this aspect of their practice because they see no imperative to deal with it anymore. In one sense this is all very predictable and understandable but I suppose the worrying side to this development is that artists can actually end up facilitating a kind of amnesia.

PS: I think that corresponds to other things that are going on in South Africa. Many people feel that it's dangerous to dwell on the past and the future simply means a sort of pursuit of cheerful individualism. We need a broader definition of the 'political'. In my own case, for me *not* to take on the issue of 'race' would be an evasion, and for all the difficulties presented by the questions of representation which we've touched on here, the absence of 'race' in my work would be as politically problematic as it would be aesthetically restrictive.

Notes

Annie E. Coombes teaches Cultural Studies and Art History at Birkbeck College, University of London. She is the author of *Reinventing Africa: Museums, Material Culture and Popular Imagination in Late Victorian and Edwardian England* (1994) Yale University Press.

Penny Siopis is Professor of Fine Art at the University of the Witwatersrand, Johannesburg, South Africa.

* This interview took place in Johannesburg in December 1994. Some changes have been made to bring it up to date with the constantly transforming situation in South Africa.

After the Ivory Tower:

Gender, commodification and the 'academic'

Joanna de Groot

FEMINIST REVIEW NO 55, SPRING 1997, pp. 130–42

Abstract

This piece uses a feminist approach to explore various aspects of 'commodification' in the lives and work of those teaching and researching in UK universities, and in particular its gender dimensions. After setting a historical context for the radical transformation of UK universities during the 1980s, it considers how this transformation was experienced by academics in terms of alienation, anxiety and accountability. Key features of that experience are loss of autonomy and control to the external power of competition and managerialism, insecurity and casualization in employment, and exposure to increasing judgemental scrutiny. For women academics job insecurity and discrimination continue to be disproportionately important, although some of the challenges to old established academic convention and practice have opened up real possibilities to progress more pro-women agendas. In the future they will confront quite depressing developments in the reconstruction of academic identities and labour, but have the legacy of the gains/insights of feminist analysis and politics over the last twenty years with which to do so.

Keywords

women; academic; gender; transformation; universities

Over the last year I've worked in the headquarters of the Association of University Teachers (AUT) dealing as an elected national officer with the impact of massive changes in academic life and work on tens of thousands of people like myself employed in universities. Each of us individually as well as collectively are engaged with what can best be described as material and cultural transformations which are reconstructing us as subjects. One way to understand such transformations is as a process of 'commodification' of our labour, our skills and our relationships to students, colleagues and our academic/intellectual/scholarly endeavours. The language of government directives and press releases says that we 'provide' teaching or research supervision to student 'consumers' rather than participating in or supporting learning, research and education which are now called 'products' or 'services'. Our decisions about topics to investigate or write about are made on the basis not of importance or interest alone, but of marketability to funding bodies, publishers or prospective employers and heads of department who can, and do, manage, censor and constrain those decisions. We are conscious of our precarious position in academic employment with the growth of short-term contracts, hourly paid work and all the attendant pressure and exploitation experienced by a casualized workforce. We are asked to describe what we do in terms of 'competencies' which are supposed to grade our skills and activities to fit the needs of managers and pay systems, rather than in terms of how we operate, develop and interact with others as scholars, teachers, investigators or analysts.

There are many perspectives on the origins, character and implications of these changes in what it means to 'be an academic' or 'do academic work'. In this discussion I want to concentrate on the gender dynamics of both the process and the experience of the changing practices, values and structures with which academics are involved. My generation is the first in which women began to enter university education and academic employment in growing numbers. It was the generation who developed new feminist analyses of society and the ideas or other means whereby we understand it, and who launched practical political initiatives based on such analyses within most of the spheres in which we lived and worked and created, including the academic world. Both daily experience and feminist understanding give us a direct and distinctive purchase (intellectual and practical) on the changes of the last two decades. Feminist evaluation of the *gendered* character of academic institutions (i.e. male dominance and power) and of academic work (i.e. gender-blind/biased and masculinist scholarly theory, method and practice) forms a key body of knowledge and critique addressing both established forms and experiences and more recent transformations in these areas. It can show how the general process of change is gendered overall, and also how some of the causes, character and consequences of change are gender-specific.

A brief historical comment will help us to understand the processes now impacting on academic institutions, practice and practitioners. Nineteenth-century developments in those spheres constructed a fabric of 'professional' knowledge, power, skill and influence located in universities and learned societies, and reaching via the educational formation of key elites into the domain of public opinion, the shaping of social consensus and control, and the management of government. In Britain, unlike elsewhere in Europe, state patronage and intervention played a somewhat limited role in these developments, so that emergent groups of 'professional' scholars/academics based in new institutions and 'disciplines' found themselves relatively marginal, albeit influential within the culture. On the one hand one points to the successful development of new forms of organized intellectual practice and practitioners towards the new status of 'science',

131

and to the role of universities in forming the imperial governing classes and sections of the intelligentsia, who by the later nineteenth century influenced significant elements of political and cultural life. On the other hand one recognizes certain persistent, widely held and hostile views; academic/scholarly activity is frequently dismissed as irrelevant or inappropriate to the 'real' needs of business, empire and social change (the 'ivory tower' view); criticism is made of the damaging challenges posed by narrow coteries of intellectuals to cherished and generally held values or commitments (i.e. elite and popular condemnations of such persons as unrepresentative, amoral, atheistical, decadent); there is even a rejection of the very processes of reasoning, investigation and analysis which underpinned and legitimized academic activity implied by the classic commonplace English phrase 'too clever by half'.

There was of course a powerfully gendered aspect to the nineteenth-century transformation/construction of academic knowledge, institutions and occupations, as there was to the consolidation of other areas of power and professionalism in business, medicine or government. Debate over the exclusion/admission of women from academic and scholarly practice entwined with gendered constructions of 'reason', 'learning' and 'science' as in various senses 'masculine', forming a core feature of the discourses and decisions which shaped the development of universities and related institutions. It combined with other constructions of social hierarchy and acceptability used to define such institutions in terms of cultural, ethnic and socio-economic privilege and its obverse, disadvantage. Those few women who gained access to academic study and employment did so in that specific context, and indeed access to education and knowledge became a key trope within middle-class female critiques of gender inequity and the 'first wave' feminist politics which emerged from it.

Studies of these processes are a frequent subject for feminist historians of the 'second wave'. However, in considering the present conjuncture in academic lives and institutions it is simply important to recognize how their development in modern times established significant and ambivalent combinations of marginality and privilege in relation to power, resources, and hierarchies, including gender power and hierarchy. Universities depended largely on public funds which were, however, channelled to them via an arms-length body, the University Grants Committee set up in 1911, rather than a government department, and had limited links with industry or market forces. Academics, with notable exceptions, often from Oxbridge, tended to be at the shabby-genteel end of the professional spectrum, respectable rather than influential. Their work reflected individualist choices and collegially enforced subject conventions, a terrain of 'freedom' subject to little scrutiny, but equally given little attention. Access to universities was limited, and functioned as a rite of passage to certain professions or to social acceptance and status in some cases, although, as work such as that of Carol Dyhouse shows, it might occasionally offer mobility for a few aspirants from underprivileged or non-establishment backgrounds, including some women. The prevailing ethos of English academia in the first half of this century was that of an undernourished professionalism (seen in the records of the Association of University Teachers founded in 1919) and a cautious liberalism confined by convention which could tolerate 1930s left dissidence without letting it have any real impact. Critical and creative intellectual endeavour were the fortunate byproducts rather than the driving vision or purpose of the system.

Changes in universities in the 1960s and 1970s reconfigured these features rather than definitively changing them. Growth in student numbers and consequently in institutions and academic jobs created a more diverse student body without ending the old patterns of class, cultural and gender bias. More significantly, the expectation of state support for student tuition and maintenance enshrined in the grant reforms of the 1960s created a potentially egalitarian commitment hard to sustain as the system grew. Meanwhile, the transformation/diversification of the academic as well as the student body brought unprecedented levels of political and cultural energy and critical edge into academia, opening up new fields of scholarship, analysis and debate on the content, purpose and delivery of research and learning. All higher education institutions experienced and contributed to the impact of forces which pushed at the boundaries of convention with initiatives ranging from the fleetingly fashionable to the genuinely innovative. Nonetheless the Robbins articulation of an updated mission/purpose for universities and its implementation embodied much that restated older liberal but hierarchical and restrictive approaches while adapting them to a more open social setting and meritocratic ethos. In keeping with the corporatist trends of the period it was state intervention which engineered the changes at institutional level, although it was critical intervention by participants in the system (staff, students) which infused creativity, optimism and controversy into its workings. The latter proved sufficiently robust to offset either governmental or market pressures which might, for example, have directed student choice towards scientific/technological rather than humanistic or social-scientific subjects. The historic pattern of distance between the academy and such pressures was maintained.

It was the period from the mid-1970s to the early 1990s which saw the dramatic shifts which opened up the university system and its denizens to much more forceful intervention by governments and 'markets'. Financial cuts first imposed in 1976 and intensified in the early 1980s forced

FEMINIST REVIEW NO 55, SPRING 1997

universities to both pressurize staff and seek new sources of income – effectively the start of the process of 'marketing' universities to conferences, to overseas students or to commercial sponsors. Government policy (driven by ideology) had a number of contradictory effects. Its drive for deregulation and competition – upheld as desirable in themselves – opened the way to rampant institutional individualism and insecurity as each university scrambled for its own share of resources, students and research funding. According to the classic Thatcherite paradox, government pursued this deregulationist policy while simultaneously reducing the influence and autonomy of intermediary forces in higher education such as the committee of vice-chancellors and the funding bodies by its financial, legislative and political intervention. In the financial domain their year-on-year pressure on public spending ended the old quinquennial pattern and broke up stable planning horizons. Legislative intervention like the 1988 Education Reform Act endowed any Minister of Education with literally hundreds of statutory powers. Short-term political convenience or ideological bias rather than considered approaches to the role and structure of higher education drove key initiatives like the 'ending' of the binary divide in 1991–2, and the unplanned, under-resourced and high-speed increase in student numbers in the late 1980s and early 1990s. These challenged the autonomy and self-referential framework of the sector by unleashing the forces of 'market'[1] competition and government intervention articulated and legitimized within a discourse/practice of public accountability, 'value for money' and external scrutiny.

So what does this mean for 'being an academic' or 'doing academic work' in the 1990s – and in particular what does it mean for women academics? Three interlocking themes suggest themselves – alienation, anxiety, accountability – each with both a general and a gender-specific dimension. By alienation I refer to the growing sense of separation between work and personal identity experienced by many academics, and to the experience of loss of control or even influence over many aspects of teaching, learning and research. In a material sense the freedom/power of individual academics to manage the quantity and content of workloads has been eroded by planning and resource constraints passing from funding councils to institutions, to departments and thence to each person's teaching timetable and research plans. The mix of teaching and research, the timing of scholarly work or new teaching initiatives, the numbers of students and how they are taught are significantly determined not by any individual academic or even collegially, but by requirements laid down by university managers, heads of department and external agencies. Material *quantities* – publication output, numbers of students taught, or funds generated – rather than intellectual or educational *qualities* are very much in the foreground of how academics and their work are valued. Since these quantities are now the indices of 'worth' and material reward (promotion, pay, job security), the criteria used to evaluate or enhance academic activity have shifted accordingly. The competitive question 'how do I/she/he do compared to others?' replaces the developmental question 'how can I/she/he improve on past work?', or the normative 'how does this work meet the aims/criteria/ideals for the subject or field?', which alienates the academic questioner both from the activities involved and from fellow practitioners, not to mention the effects on peer judgement, etc.

There is of course a well-established feminist critique of the competitive, individualist and output-oriented aspects of academic life and activity and their links to male privilege, which draws attention to the value of co-operative, collective and process-oriented ways of working developed by women in the academy. The growth of the former trends has reinforced the disadvantages of women in an academic setting where such male-dominated approaches are strengthened by the professional materialism and managerialism in which male colleagues have established historic advantages. The female academic who co-operates with colleagues rather than focusing solely on career opportunities for herself, or who does unquantified/unrewarded work which doesn't 'count' (in either sense of the term), or who has staggered her career to meet commitments to dependants or partners, may well find her 'score' on the new indices unfavourably affected. This long-established problem, evident in the striking gender imbalance in promotion prospects which disadvantages women academics, is likely to intensify in the climate of 1990s academia. In 1993–4 figures, women form only 23 per cent of academics and researchers (less in many science subjects) and are concentrated on lower grades and in short-term or part-time posts often funded by 'soft' money. As such their opportunity to identify as full/equal members of the academic community, let alone play an equal role in shaping that community, has been sharply affected by their gender, and by the unpopularity attendant on raising gender issues (as with other equality issues such as race and class) in the academy. It is ironic that at the very point when effective argument and campaigning by academics, notably women, through AUT succeeded in creating pressure for the establishment of the CVCP's[2] Committee on University Career Opportunity with a specific remit to address discrimination, new trends may actually reinforce discrimination.

Just as the material forces reshaping academic work and careers have produced alienation among academics, so too have the power relations flowing from the managerialism which has spread through universities over the last fifteen years. It emerged in response to government pressures on university planning and resources, to ideological demands for universities to run 'efficiently' on 'business' principles, and to political pressure for transparency and accountability in the academy. As a result many areas of choice, strategy and decision-making are now driven by institutional plans and policies determined centrally by small groups of powerful individuals rather than by academics individually or collegially. Such restricted circles of power and control in universities are male-dominated if not all-male, as shown by statistics on the professoriat, departmental heads, and especially on deans, pro-vice-chancellors and their equivalents. Thus the decline of collegiality and democratic governance in universities, accelerated by external imperatives from the Jarrett 'reforms' to the current funding and quality mechanisms, again has a gendered twist with women typically excluded from power and influence to a greater degree than men. Individual talented and/or ambitious women have of course breached the barriers on occasion, which throws into relief the alienation which is likely to be the experience of the majority.

If alienation springs from the experience of material and political inequity and exclusion from resources, power and opportunity, anxiety springs from the articulation of that exclusion with all the job and professional insecurity created by growing competition, marketization and scarce resources deployed by unregulated managements. Such insecurity is of course a widespread trend in employment in the UK, although newer, and so more sharply experienced in some sectors, including professional ones, than others. In universities the growth of casualization through fixed-term and part-time work among academic staff is a significant recent phenomenon. Over one-third of academic staff are contract researchers, the majority on contracts of two years or less; there are now thousands of lecturing staff on short fixed-term contracts, while the decade 1983/4 to 1993/4 saw a *71 per cent increase* in staff on part-time pro-rata contracts (that is some fraction of a full-time contract) with other increases in part-time hourly paid jobs. These developments have included a noticeable feminization of casual academic work. A 1995 survey of AUT members showed that while 16.2 per cent of male respondents were on fixed-term contracts, the figure for women was 31 per cent. Part-time work in particular, both in lecturing and research, typically involves more women than men, and the perennial issue of career breaks for family commitments gives a further gendered dynamic to casualization.

Quite apart from the material difficulties imposed by insecure employment there are other serious sources of anxiety for those in temporary or part-time work which reconfigure the various meanings of academic work and identity. These range from the time taken from teaching, research and scholarship to seek new posts or grants to the forms of legal discrimination in employment rights (including maternity rights) and exclusion from institutional or departmental facilities, participation and democratic processes. Rather than having confidence in their place in the academy alongside fellow scholars and professionals, the casualized academic workforce has to focus on 'marketing' themselves not only to potential employers or fund providers but also to fellow academics. Such academics stand in relations of power and patronage to their fixed-term or part-time colleagues and are themselves responsible for part of the discriminatory treatment experienced by those colleagues. While these elements of hierarchy and power are of course well-established features of academic life, they have been intensified by the dramatic expansion of impermanent employment to cover getting on for half of those in academic jobs. The resultant anxiety operates on at least three levels; first, any individual in insecure employment has practical fears about their material future; second, the unequal rights and status of those in such employment puts them at a personal/political disadvantage on the terrain of professional and institutional life; third, the experience of belonging to or identification with the academy and academic colleagues with greater security is undermined by this personal material and political disfranchisement, and the persistent competition and migration, which also weaken the fragile collegiality and solidarity within the academic community.

This anxiety and alienation have been given greater force by the enforced emergence of academics and their activities from the semi-darkness of craft mystery (or mystification!) into the light of accountability. In the past devising and delivering university courses, assessing students and shaping research and writing were activities which academics assumed they would be left alone to pursue, judged, validated and legitimated only by their peers acting as external examiners, assessors of research proposals, scholarly reviewers, patrons and departmental critics. Over the last two decades scarcity of resources and consequent difficulties in allocating them have brought financial considerations more into play in the support of research and in decisions about creating, delivering or recruiting for new courses. Moreover a challenging critique of the assumption that academic activity (teaching, learning, assessment, research) was an arcane mystery, comprehensible and assessable solely by professional practitioners, was coming into play. This critique drew on the arguments of those in the academy (students, junior staff) and outside observers who were excluded from the arena of peer judgement and mystified as to the evidence for its rationality and justice. Such arguments converged with the politico-ideological agenda of governments in the 1980s which focused on reducing the autonomy and privileges of professionals, drawing on popular/populist suspicion of the activities and perquisites of academics, seen, not without reason, as beneficiaries and agents of an elitist, unaccountable and 'irrelevant' system.

Pressure on scarce resources, questioning of academic self-assessment, and government-sponsored intervention combined to produce demands for 'value for money', and for transparency and accountability for the standards and quality of academic activity. The elaborate bureaucracies of quality assurance and research assessment, and the role of external evaluation are the material manifestations of that process.

The process of 'accounting' (in all senses!) for academic work has reached into the labour process itself with the growth of appraisal systems, staff development programmes, and the use of performance related and discretionary rewards. The effects of these have been complex. Academics have been able to use appraisal processes to claim due recognition for their achievements and needs, and in the case of women to challenge some of the conventional masculinist definitions of these and to assert their claims for advancement with greater confidence. Through their union they have used collective bargaining to claim a role in the process and shared training and experience to support members and combat discrimination. Performance-related and discretionary pay have also been brought within a framework of negotiation. Equally these interventions in the conduct and payment of academic work have created a culture of scrutiny which both expresses valid demands for academic accountability and effectiveness, and also operates by means of imposition and accusations (actual or implied) of deficiency or incompetence based on a particular style of management rather than evidence. Just as the quality assessment of teaching has paid no more than lip service to the developmental and enhancement as opposed to the judgemental side of the matter, so reorganization of courses and teaching time (modularization and semesterization) has been dominated by financial or managerial imperatives rather than educational or intellectual ones. Now at last the very composition of academic work is being taken apart for scrutiny in an attempt to create 'maps' of the 'functions' of higher education and descriptions of 'competencies' which could be used to determine academic pay and promotion as well as professional formation and development. Activities which depend for their very effectiveness on integrating complex areas of knowledge, skill and experience, and on combining educational, intellectual and interpersonal work, are being fragmented into checklists of criteria and categories to be ticked off. What passes for analysis of how academics work is in fact an approach which arguably by its very nature will fail to be so.

Arguably too this kind of fragmentation may open up possibilities for shifting conventional assumptions and practices which have biased the recognition of academic work and worth against women and other marginalized or underprivileged categories of academics. Here we should balance the positive opportunities created by the very existence of a debate about what research and teaching actually are with a certain realism about how that will be shaped by vested interests, financial necessities and political considerations. Experience of arguing, as I think rightly, against a 'competencies' analysis of research and teaching while also arguing for a non-discriminatory approach to these activities has shown me that although it is worth seizing the chance to challenge masculinist bias, one conducts the argument on competencies alongside those whose opposition is rooted in gendered vested interest. More generally one should note that the resistance of much of the academic community to the new culture of scrutiny and accountability combines valid criticisms of that culture with opposition to precisely the scrutiny to which feminists and others troubled by the monocultural inequities of the academy have long wished to subject it.

Here we come to one of the core issues confronting women in the academy and feminist approaches to academic life and work. Over the last twenty-five years diversification among students and staff and the opening up of new areas or forms of teaching, learning, research and scholarship have usefully challenged fixed, simple and one-dimensional conceptions of 'an academic', 'a subject', or even 'a university'. In that sense the deconstruction and fragmentation of our understanding of academic work, or institutions, or the people involved in them have had real benefits for the marginalized, misrepresented and excluded sections of the academic community, as also in other social settings. However, since diversification and deconstruction have been accompanied by and interacted with growing material and political inequity and insecurity, their liberating effects within the academy have been significantly constrained and even reversed. Justifiable resistance to Thatcherite political attacks, to the endless competition for declining resources, and to cultural/ideological challenges to academic practice and precepts has taken the form of defending professional practice, values and identity, including some of those less defensible characteristics challenged by feminists. Moreover, as individuals and institutions experience direct threats to their material interests they have devoted more energy to dealing with such threats than to sustaining liberating and progressive developments toward equity and plurality. Protest and conservatism have gone hand in hand, whether in campaigns on excessive workloads which foreground secure male academics at the expense of their casualized, often female, colleagues, or in explicit arguments that anti-discrimination issues should 'of course' take a back seat in these times of redundancy and attack.

For those of us who think that such issues, among which gender discrimination is vital, are still central, and indeed a necessary component of any resistance to the damage being done to staff, students and universities, some difficult decisions loom close. Just as we have engaged with the challenge of dealing with gender identities, interests and inequities along-side others which may both conflict and converge with them, so now we confront the task of sustaining a gender critique of the academy while also resisting other critiques beside allies who do not support our gender agenda. As with class, ethnic or community politics so the politics of our academic future involve choices that are neither clear nor simple if that agenda is to be sustained. Here I take comfort from the evidence that many women colleagues are bringing either the confidence and knowledge of twenty years of gender politics, or the confidence of inheriting that legacy as younger women, to the current struggles (material and cultural) over what it is to be an academic or 'do' academic work. Among those I work with in AUT I find little willingness to accept that our current difficulties can be addressed by back-tracking on gender issues and interests. They see themselves as negotiating alliances in which advancing such issues and interests form part of the commitment to resist attacks on jobs and insti-tutions. In the area of academic practice whether in scholarship, teaching or research they have argued persuasively against untenable defences of a discriminatory status quo and made the case for reconstructing 'best prac-tice' incorporating critiques of discrimination and marginalization. Without giving too rosy a picture it is accurate and important to note how women and feminists in the academy have responded creatively (under stress!), and combined continuing commitment to change its historic bias and inequities, with commitment to resist the inroads of insecurity and alienation. They don't throw babies out with bathwater.

Part of our ability to maintain this creative combination comes precisely from feminist thought and politics. Feminism's grasp of the politics of per-sonal relations, of the intimate as well as the institutional locations of power, and of the complex interaction of material and cultural dimensions in human experience and social structures is directly relevant. It can inform a serious critique of currently influential views of students as 'consumers' or education as a 'product', just as they contribute to views on quality assurance or promotion which neither endorse unacceptable old ways of doing things, nor collude with destructive new proposals. It allows us to advance a perspective on academic 'values' or professional practice which rejects their disparagement in the name of efficiency, marketability or anti-intellectualism, but also their use to justify elitism and exclusion. It enables us to think through and act on an analysis of the costs and benefits of alliances, even where this is quite painful.

Women and feminists in universities find themselves in a paradoxical, con-tradictory situation. The 'gender agenda' of challenge to established aca-demic structures, conventions and institutions, which aims both to bring women into the academy as constituted *and* to reconstitute it, has been among the forces which are deconstructing historic notions of 'the academic'. However, proponents of that agenda do not in general support those other forces of deconstruction which have been described earlier in this paper, and indeed may well be damaged by them. While we may be clear that a return to past structures and practices is undesirable even if it were possible (which it isn't), we are much less clear about how to reconstruct academic life, work and values in the context of attacks on many aspects of these which are valuable as opposed to those which are not. Just as it is difficult for academics to find the most effective and relevant blend of trade union and professional response to market competition, cultural displacement and power politics, so feminist responses are caught between gender analysis and politics and other professional, social or political commitments. Perhaps our advantage in this situation is that we have relevant past experience to draw on, in that much feminist politics has dealt with the negotiation of difficult, multiple, conflicting interests or identities. We confront commodification and cultural power in the academic sphere with the benefit of our analysis and experience of those processes in the sphere of gender relations and inequalities, which yields some interesting ironies when some of us have to deal with the commodification of gender and feminist scholarship!

In a discussion which has followed a train of thought rather than providing a full-scale analysis it is difficult to make an ending, if only because each stage of thinking stimulates further questions and reflections. Nonetheless I think it is fitting to end on a note of paradox. It is easy, even reasonable, to be pessimistic about any change in the agenda which currently dominates the reconstruction of academic institutions, practices and identities, and about whether conservative resistance to that agenda can be shifted towards creative reconstruction. However, it would be unreasonable and unhistorical to ignore other features of our situation; there are positive as well as negative dimensions to the deconstruction of the historic forms and relationships of academe; the possibility of creative alliances and initiatives among those who challenge the dominant agenda, albeit from positions of relative powerlessness, not only exists but sometimes emerges into actuality; specifically the development of debate and politics around the Dearing enquiry should be taken seriously. The sheer range and diversity of interested parties in the politics of higher education may be uncomfortable for academics accustomed to self-regulation, but it opens up opportunities for alliances as much as threats to autonomy, the possibility of moving from marginality to something more fruitful. Rather than forecasting any outcome (pessimistic or optimistic), it seems more useful to encourage reflection and action which can actually affect the outcome.

Joanna de Groot teaches in the history department and the Centre for Women's Studies at York University. Her main academic interests are in socio-cultural histories of the interaction of gender with other interests, experiences and subjectivities in women's lives and politics globally over the last two centuries. She is also involved in political and trade union activity inside and outside the academy, and has been active nationally in the Association of University Teachers for the last ten years, including serving as national President during 1995–6.

1 This term has a more complex signification for higher education than there is space to explore here.
2 The Committee of Vice-Chancellors and Principals (heads of HE institutions in the UK).

Reviews

FEMINIST REVIEW NO 55, SPRING 1997, pp. 143–9

Fear of the Dark: 'Race', Gender and Sexuality in the Cinema
Lola Young
Routledge: London, 1996
ISBN 0 415 19710 X

Published in Routledge's 'Gender, Racism, Ethnicity' series, Lola Young's book is a long awaited study of intersecting representations of 'race', gender, class and sexuality in British cinema. As such, it fills a hitherto frustrating gap in both British film studies and black feminist criticism. Whilst the suggestion that *Fear of the Dark* extends beyond such remits would remain within the terms of a discourse of 'race' which Young has so effectively repositioned, *Fear of the Dark* is relevant not only to analysis of representations of 'race' and gender in British film, but to any cultural analysis.

Identity politics, through which black, feminist and lesbian criticism initially developed, has become at odds with text-based analysis. Psychoanalysis, which is central to feminist film-studies, has always been a source of critical ambivalence for black people, lesbians, gays and feminists. It has also been seen as inconsistent with *any* historically situated critique. Young has achieved a persuasively coherent integration of black feminist perspectives with post-structuralist and historically recontextualized psychoanalytic techniques.

Young's opening chapters engage with discourses of 'race', representation and spectatorship. Previous studies have tended towards a reductionist analysis of stereotyping, revealing a continued reliance on essentialist concepts: for example, seeing 'bucks' and 'whores' behind every attractive black actor's performance, as though such stereotypes and their meanings were universal. Black filmmaking has been evaluated in terms of its effectiveness as a 'window on the (black) world'. Young argues that any images of black people can, instead, be read as tropes

FEMINIST REVIEW NO 55, SPRING 1997

evolving from the complex ' "master" discourses of colonialism', which need to be historicized, with a view to identifying shifting themes and metaphors (p. 9).

Next, Young examines discourses of gender. Often analysis of gender and sexuality has been absent from black criticism; and even when critics such as Pines (1981) do note that black women and men are differentially inscribed in British films, analysis has not been developed. White feminist film-studies has also under-analysed 'racialization'. Where 'race' has been addressed, there has been a 'privileging of gender as the locus of oppression' (p. 17). Young argues for, and from, a feminist perspective which needs to:

> identify the extent to which gender and sexuality may be seen as racialized discourses in the cinema. . . . The ways in which texts by both black and white film-makers indicate contrasting notions of black and white femininities . . .
>
> (p. 13)

It is Young's mode of repositioning discourses of gender and sexuality which is crucial to the far-reaching implications of Young's thesis for feminism, film and cultural studies generally.

Young applies the complexities of this rigorous reading strategy to British cinema with absorbing results. Organized within a historical schema, shifts and persistences in the intersecting discourses of 'race', gender, sexuality and class take shape through readings exploring the problematization of the black family, anxieties surrounding interracial sexuality, and exoticization in 1950s and 1960s mainstream films such as *Sapphire* (1959), *Flame in the Streets* (1961), and *Leo the Last* (1969); treatment of similar issues and of critical issues surrounding black filmmaking in *Pressure* (1974) and *Burning an Illusion* (1981); and the reworking of the 'racialization' of white, male sexual anxieties in *Mona Lisa* (1986).

In terms of my own critical agendas, whilst Young's repositioning of gender discourse radically expands possibilities for black and white lesbian critical approaches, her own analysis of an interrelation of 'racialized' and 'transgressive' sexualities from earlier chapters (p. 22–32) remains rather underdeveloped.

Black women as critics, spectators and filmmakers also rather haunt the margins of Young's conclusion. Young is centrally concerned with a more critically effective engagement with discursive practices of 'race' and gender. The displacement of the false coherence of essentializing categories such as 'race' tends however, to produce a hiatus in which the act of speaking '*as*' (?) is held in tension with a critical displacement of any subject position(s) from which one may speak coherently. The question of what it means to engage *as* a marginal 'reader' or 'speaker' can only shift to the historical plane, or become inarticulate. This complex question, raised in the opening chapters (p. 10), is not substantially addressed. Young has, however, cleared a terrain on which such a debate may move beyond a 'counter-mythologizing' tendency; and on which white feminists may also begin to develop a more effective engagement with the racialization of discourses of gender and sexuality. The value of Young's critical method to a wide range of oppositional critical practices lies, not least, in her commitment.

> [Not to] . . . construct a hierarchy of oppression but to suggest that a more reflective critical practice needs to be developed in order to analyse the complex ways in which these systems of oppression may be destabilized.
>
> (p. 177)

Paula Graham

References

PINES, Jim (1981) 'Blacks in film: the British angle' *Multi-racial Education* Vol. 9, No. 2, Spring.

Resident Alien: Feminist Cultural Criticism
Janet Wolff
Polity Press: Cambridge, 1995
ISBN 0 7456 1250 4, £39.50 Hbk ISBN 0 74556 1251 2, £11.95 Pbk

'Do foreigners make the best sociologists?' Wolff provocatively asks in her opening line and in as much as Wolff now describes herself as a 'resident alien', Professor of Art History at the University of Rochester, the answer after reading these essays is a resounding yes (p. 1). *Resident Alien* builds on Wolff's earlier work, *The Social Production of Art* and *Feminine Sentences*, and similarly offers a historical and discursively feminist account of aspects of modernity (Walter Benjamin, the *flâneur* and the painter Gwen John) as well as chapters on popular music of the 1950s.

Travel, women's marginality, and, borrowing a phrase from Jane Tompkins, 'the move towards the memoiristic' are themes that recur throughout the essays as well as a continuing interest in 'personal criticism' as a vehicle for intellectual analysis.

Wolff offers new insights into what Gayatri Spivak has called the 'winning back' of the position of the questioning subject or what Wolff herself calls

FEMINIST REVIEW NO 55, SPRING 1997

a 'sociology of the marginal' (Spivak, 1990: 42; Wolff, 1995: 2). What this involves in the opening chapter, for example, is a carefully positioned account of travelling women intellectuals including women of the Left Bank, contemporary Americans such as Alice Kaplan as well as Wolff herself, an account which neither romanticizes exile nor freezes exile historically. *Resident Alien*, like the best contemporary feminist writing, has been transformed by interest in theories of the subject, critiques of historiography and the boundaries between disciplines exemplified in Wolff's wonderfully titled chapter 'Eddie Cochran, Donna Anna and the Dark Sister: Personal Experience and Cultural History'. Long gone is the notion that criticism involves appreciating gender neutral art and cultural products. Feminism has altered the whole framework of criticism introducing complex models of viewers/readers which defy formalist efforts to ignore gender, race and other differences.

Wolff's engaging, non-assertive rhetoric, full of 'it is not possible to give a generic answer', 'I think', 'my suggestions', vividly explores the gaps between cultural processes of identity construction and her own life history (and love of Eddie Cochran). Sometimes this means that Wolff vectors through too many cultural 'degrees'. For example, in a typical double page we read about Bizet's *Carmen*, Tony Harrison's *Bow Down*, Richard Dyer on Marilyn Monroe, being Jewish in a Christian culture, Sander Gilman, Klaus Thewelweit, Susan Bordo and the killing of a plastic surgeon and hairdresser in Chicago. A fascinating journey in which Wolff's own meridian or magnetic pole is not clear.

Perhaps it is because Wolff repeatedly delivered these essays as public lectures that they are at one and the same time analytical and dialogic. It seems to me that Wolff's work joins the new, or newly visible, body of feminist memoiristic writing in Britain which is intensely self-reflexive, carefully exact historically, multigeneric, wide ranging in its references but simultaneously intimate in its address to the reader and sometimes passionately dialogic. I am thinking here, for example, of Lauretta Ngcobo's Black cultural studies, Annette Kuhn's film theory, Sally Alexander's historical essays, Carolyn Steedman's autobiography, Maud Sulter's Black aesthetics, Jeanette Winterson's art essays and the sad but bright pole star text of last year, Gillian Rose's *Love's Work*. All share that quality of directly *speaking-to* a reader of cultural complexities.

It is precisely because Wolff's style is so engaging that the book's absences are more marked. I wish that Wolff's revisiting of her germinal account of *flâneurie*, 'The invisible flâneuse' (1985), reprinted in *Feminine Sentences*, was a more sustained analysis. The original essay was an influential account of women's lack of public space, of street walking/gazing or *flâneurie*, in modernity. *Resident Alien* merely continues Wolff's earlier theme that the *flâneur* is masculine 'to say that women come to have acceptable reasons to be in the street is not to identify them as *flâneuses*' (p. 102). Yet, as Mica Nava's insightful topoi of feminine modernity points out, Wolff's argument ignores women's everyday experience of the city, particularly that of working women and indeed that modernity rapidly expanded what counted as respectable public space for women including the cinema, the department store and transport (Nava, 1996).

Wolff also treats too sparingly one of the most powerful influences on feminist aesthetics and practice in the 1980s: the engagement with psycho-analysis and its transformation of notions of female identity which continues into the 1990s in the writing of Bracha Lichtenberg-Ettinger (Humm, forthcoming). More problematic is Wolff's avoidance of the complexities of ethnicity and sexualities; in particular, how Black criticism, for example Maud Sulter's *Passion*, challenges white representations of women's cultural practices (Sulter, 1990). Addressing Black and Third World perspectives would have helped Wolff to rethink her central theme of travelling. For example, Maria Lugones describes travelling as a way of experiencing *differences* by shifting into a different space of being (Lugones, 1987).

There *are* silences in *Resident Alien* but Wolff's vivid voice speaking of that complex interaction between female identity (if not identities) and culture manages to talk us through historiography, cultural theory and memoir into a feminist cultural sociology which never feels foreign.

Maggie Humm

References

HUMM, Maggie (forthcoming) *Feminism and Film* Edinburgh: Edinburgh University Press.

LUGONES, Maria (1987) 'Playfulness, "world"-travelling, and loving perception' *Hypatia: a Journal of Feminist Philosophy* Vol. 2, No. 2: 3–9.

NAVA, Mica (1996) 'Modernity's disavowal: women, the city and the department store in **Nava** and **Shea**, editors *Modern Times: Reflections on a Century of English Modernity* London: Routledge.

SPIVAK, Gayatri C. (1990) *The Postcolonial Critic: Interviews, Strategies, Dialogues* London: Routledge.

SULTER, Maud (ed.) (1990) *Passion: Discourses on Black Women's Creativity* Hebden Bridge: Urban Fox Press.

Imperial Leather: Race, Gender and Sexuality in the Colonial Contest

Anne McClintock

Routledge: London, 1995

ISBN 0 415 90890 6, £13.99 Pbk, ISBN 0 415 90889 2, £37.50 Hbk

This is a huge and delightful book which I enjoyed immensely. McClintock's project, which is to trace the constitutive intersections of gender, nation, class and race whilst arguing for the importance of the cultural, is brave and will offer much to readers in its various fields. The ways in which categories of racial difference are implicitly and explicitly gendered and in which gender difference is always racialized are skillfully dissected in the diverse realms of nationalism, commodity fetishism, literature and political activity. McClintock takes the European cult of domesticity as her theme, and uses it to discuss the essential but marginalized female labour (waged and unwaged) that materially and symbolically underpinned the development of imperial and capital relations as we recognize them today.

Her commitment to recognizing women's agency in power relations where other commentators often simply don't see it is also to be welcomed. That she does this without needing to present women as pure heroines untainted by any complicity in social power relations, even as they may be oppressed to varying extents in terms of gender, is excellent: whether she is discussing white working-class women servants in nineteenth-century Britain, black women servants in South Africa or black or white women's autobiography, McClintock attends to the specific ways in which different women are themselves implicated in the constituent terms of those differentiations. Thus, she can write about Hannah Cullwick's cross class relationship with Arthur Munby without shirking the imperialism and racism that structures their fantasy life and talk about the different but equally complex racializing of gender relations and gendering of race relations in post-Boer War Afrikaner society and the 1990s ANC. By turning her attention to formations of all political hues and different historical moments, McClintock is able to suggest the infinitely variable balance of payments that can lead to the sorts of sexual and colonial ambivalences that have been so discussed of late. It is one of McClintock's best contributions that she combines an insistence on women's agency with an overarching understanding of the motivational force of sexualized pleasures. Her inscription of a female libidinal economy into a field that often regards women as only the hapless victims of male lusts produces both a new reading of familiar material and a differently constituted archive. Few readers will be equally familiar with every area she discusses: indeed, to some extent the actual range of examples must be fairly random, everyone could nominate other equally fertile texts or moments. But McClintock knows her material and weaves it together well.

In addition to several case studies in the literary field (Haggard, Schreiner, Black South African poets in the 1950s and 1970s) McClintock also includes the production and consumption of material culture. She investigates soap manufacture and advertising in the late nineteenth and early twentieth centuries to demonstrate how imperial culture touched every area of daily life. In a welcome addition to existing work in the field of imperial spectacle and popular imperialism, McClintock shows how the visuals of advertising brought imperial iconographies into casual contact with the whole British population, illustrating how imperial cultures reached well beyond the elite.

McClintock has produced some of the most intelligent writing on sado-masochism of recent years and her analysis of the multi-faceted impact of fetishism (sexual, commodity and racial) in colonial and postcolonial lives is invaluable. Although I am not entirely persuaded by her analysis of the Cull-wick/Munby archive, I am wholly persuaded by her insistence that women's social agency can also be sexualized. In all her examples, McClintock demonstrates a willingness to go out on a limb in both her grouping of material and her conclusions on it. That this originality is combined with a thoroughly scholarly protocol makes this a particularly valuable book. Her research is extensive and the footnotes and references will in themselves be helpful to many readers, as will her overview of current work in each field.

If the book has a weakness, it is that in her desire to include everything, McClintock covers too much and leaves hostages to fortune with some of the less extensive case studies. It is a fault that I can easily forgive (not just because I am prone to it myself) but because none of her inclusions detract from her overall argument; they merely threaten to distract the reader away from their original purpose and into other equally provocative areas. If you are not reading this book from cover to cover for review purposes, then don't let its size put you off: feel free to dip in. You won't be bored. The book is clearly written in a lively accessible style with a clear commitment to political change that brings home the 'real life' implications of each example. Her engagement with political and cultural theorists from Freud to Fanon and from Kristeva to Sheila Jeffries provides a neat synthesis of many of cultural studies' preoccupations for the past decade. This, along with her own insights and a demonstrable desire to harness cultural analysis to social change, should be one in the eye for those who have recently panned cultural studies as an other-worldly, ivory-tower indulgence.

Reina Lewis

Noticeboard

FEMINIST REVIEW NO 55, SPRING 1997, pp. 150–1

Call for Papers

Women's History Network
6th Annual Conference: 'Voices, Narratives, Identities'
Saturday 13 and Sunday 14 September 1997, University of Sussex.
Offers of Papers by 21 March 1997 to:

Gerry Holloway/Pat Owen, Education Development Building, University of Sussex, Falmer, Brighton, BN1 9RG.
Please mark your envelope 'WHN'.

Call for Papers

Women's Studies Network (UK) Association
10th International Conference: 'Women, Policy and Politics' 14–17 July 1997, in association with the Institute of Education, University of London

Citizenship: migration, refugees, nationalities, employment, European Union, education, law, disabilities, families . . . *Women's Movement:* activism, history, backlash, femocrats, women's studies, queer politics, religion, ecofeminism . . . *Global Change:* militarism, war zones, conflict, individualization, IT, media, marketization, time-space . . . *Health and Welfare:* mental health, reproductive rights, aging, illness, poverty, diet, addiction, lifestyles, consumption, housing . . . *Environment:* tourism, travel, violence, imprisonment, surveillance, crime, architecture . . . *Culture:* 'high' art, popular culture, science, sport, heritage, literature, spirituality . . . *Social Programme*

To receive further information on the conference, please contact The Conference Office, Institute of Education, University of London, 20 Bedford Way, London WC1; tel.: 0171 612 6017; e-mail: c.bird@ioe.ac.uk

Conference organizers: Suki Ali, Kelly Coate Bignell, Wangui Wa Goro, Diana Leonard

Please submit an abstract of 150 words for 30 minute papers on any subject relevant to the theme of the conference and items for the social programme by 30 April 1997 to: The Conference Organizers, WSN(UK)A Conference, CCS, Institute of Education, 20 Bedford Way, London WC1H 0AL; tel.: 0171 612 6245; fax: 0171 612 6177; e-mail: d.leonard@ioe.ac.uk

FEMINIST REVIEW NO 55, SPRING 1997, pp. 152–60

1 Women and Revolution in South Yemen, **Molyneux**. Feminist Art Practice, **Davis & Goodall**. Equal Pay and Sex Discrimination, **Snell**. Female Sexuality in Fascist Ideology, **Macciocchi**. Charlotte Brontë's *Shirley*, **Taylor**. Christine Delphy, **Barrett & McIntosh**. OUT OF PRINT.

2 Summer Reading, **O'Rourke**. Disaggregation, **Campaign for Legal & Financial Independence** and **Rights of Women**. The Hayward Annual 1978, **Pollock**. Women and the Cuban Revolution, **Murray**. Matriarchy Study Group Papers, **Lee**. Nurseries in the Second World War, **Riley**.

3 English as a Second Language, **Naish**. Women as a Reserve Army of Labour, **Bruegel**. Chantal Akerman's films, **Martin**. Femininity in the 1950s, **Birmingham Feminist History Group**. On Patriarchy, **Beechey**. Board School Reading Books, **Davin**.

4 Protective Legislation, **Coyle**. Legislation in Israel, **Yuval-Davis**. On 'Beyond the Fragments', *Wilson* Queen Elizabeth I, **Heisch**. Abortion Politics: **a dossier**. Materialist Feminism, **Delphy**.

5 Feminist Sexual Politics, **Campbell**. Iranian Women, **Tabari**. Women and Power, **Stacey & Price**. Women's Novels, **Coward**. Abortion, **Himmelweit**. Gender and Education, **Nava**. Sybilla Aleramo, **Caesar**. On 'Beyond the Fragments', **Margolis**.

6 'The Tidy House', **Steedman**. Writings on Housework, **Kaluzynska**. The Family Wage, **Land**. Sex and Skill, **Phillips & Taylor**. Fresh Horizons, **Lovell**. Cartoons, **Hay**.

7 Protective Legislation, Humphries. **Feminists Must Face the Future**, Coultas. **Abortion in Italy**, Caldwell. **Women's Trade Union Conferences**, Breitenbach. **Women's Employment in the Third World**, Elson & Pearson.

8 Socialist Societies Old and New, Molyneux. **Feminism and the Italian Trade Unions**, Froggett & Torchi. **Feminist Approach to Housing in Britain**, Austerberry & Watson. **Psychoanalysis**, Wilson. **Women in the Soviet Union**, Buckley. **The Struggle within the Struggle**, Kimble.

9 Position of Women in Family Law, Brophy & Smart. **Slags or Drags**, Cowie & Lees. **The Ripper and Male Sexuality**, Hollway. The Material of Male Power, **Cockburn**. Freud's *Dora*, **Moi**. Women in an Iranian Village, **Afshar**. New Office Technology and Women, **Morgall**.

Montgomery. 'Correct Distance' a photo-text, **Tabrizian**. Julia Kristeva on Femininity, **Jones**. Feminism and the Theatre, **Wandor**. Alexis Hunter, **Osborne**. Format Photographers, Dear Linda, **Kuhn**.

19 The Female Nude in the work of Suzanne Valadon, **Betterton**. Refuges for Battered Women, **Pahl**. Thin is the Feminist Issue, **Diamond**. New Portraits for Old, **Martin** & **Spence**.

20 Prisonhouses, **Steedman**. Ethnocentrism and Socialist Feminism, **Barrett** & **McIntosh**. What Do Women Want? **Rowbotham**. Women's Equality and the European Community, **Hoskyns**. Feminism and the Popular Novel of the 1890s, **Clarke**.

21 Going Private: The Implications of Privatization for Women's Work, **Coyle**. A Girl Needs to Get Street-wise: Magazines for the 1980s, **Winship**. Family Reform in Socialist States: The Hidden Agenda, Molyneux. Sexual Segregation in the Pottery Industry, **Sarsby**.

22 Interior Portraits: Women, Physiology and the Male Artist, **Pointon**. The Control of Women's Labour: The Case of Homeworking, **Allen** & **Wolkowitz**. Homeworking: Time for Change, **Cockpit Gallery** & **Londonwide Homeworking Group**. Feminism and Ideology: The Terms of Women's Stereotypes, **Seiter**. Feedback: Feminism and Racism, **Ramazanoglu, Kazi, Lees, Safia Mirza**.

23 **Socialist-feminism: out of the blue**
Feminism and Class Politics: A Round-Table Discussion, **Barrett, Campbell, Philips, Weir** & **Wilson**. Upsetting an Applecart: Difference, Desire and Lesbian Sadomasochism, **Ardill** & **O'Sullivan**. Armagh and Feminist Strategy, **Loughran**. Transforming Socialist-Feminism: The Challenge of Racism, **Bhavnani** & **Coulson**. Socialist-Feminists and Greenham, **Finch** & **Hackney Greenham Groups**. Socialist-Feminism and the Labour Party: Some Experiences from Leeds, **Perrigo**. Some Political Implications of Women's Involvement in the Miners' Strike, 1984–85, **Rowbotham** & **McCrindle**. Sisterhood: Political Solidarity Between Women, **Hooks**. European Forum of Socialist-Feminists, **Lees** & **McIntosh**. Report from Nairobi, **Hendessi**.

24 Women Workers in New Industries in Britain, **Glucksmann**. The Relationship of Women to Pornography, **Bower**. The Sex Discrimination Act 1975, **Atkins**. The Star Persona of Katharine Hepburn, **Thumim**.

25 Difference: A Special Third World Women Issue, **Minh-ha**. Melanie Klein, Psychoanalysis and Feminism, **Sayers**. Rethinking Feminist Attitudes Towards Mothering, **Gieve**. EEOC v. Sears, Roebuck and Company: A Personal Account, **Kessler-Harris**. Poems, **Wood**. Academic Feminism and the Process of De-radicalization, **Currie** & **Kazi**. A Lover's Distance: A Photoessay, **Boffin**.

26 Resisting Amnesia: Feminism, Painting and Post-Modernism, **Lee.** The Concept of Difference, **Barrett.** The Weary Sons of Freud, **Clément.** Short Story, **Cole.** Taking the Lid Off: Socialist Feminism in Oxford, **Collette.** For and Against the European Left: Socialist Feminists Get Organized, **Benn.** Women and the State: A Conference of Feminist Activists, **Weir.**

27 Women, feminism and the third term
Women and Income Maintenance, **Lister.** Women in the Public Sector, **Phillips.** Can Feminism Survive a Third Term?, **Loach.** Sex in Schools, **Wolpe.** Carers and the Careless, **Doyal.** Interview with Diane Abbott, **Segal.** The Problem With No Name: Re-reading Friedan, **Bowlby.** Second Thoughts on the Second Wave, **Rosenfelt & Stacey.** Nazi Feminists?, **Gordon.**

28 Family secrets: child sexual abuse
Introduction to an Issue: Family Secrets as Public Drama, **McIntosh.** Challenging the Orthodoxy: Towards a Feminist Theory and Practice, **MacLeod & Saraga.** The Politics of Child Sexual Abuse: Notes from American History, **Gordon.** What's in a Name?: Defining Child Sexual Abuse, **Kelly.** A Case, **Anon.** Defending Innocence: Ideologies of Childhood, **Kitzinger.** Feminism and the Seductiveness of the 'Real Event', **Scott.** Cleveland and the Press: Outrage and Anxiety in the Reporting of Child Sexual Abuse, **Nava.** Child Sexual Abuse and the Law, **Woodcraft.** Poem, **Betcher.** Brixton Black Women's Centre: Organizing on Child Sexual Abuse, **Bogle.** Bridging the Gap: Glasgow Women's Support Project, **Bell & MacLeod.** Claiming Our Status as Experts: Community Organizing, **Norwich Consultants on Sexual Violence.** Islington Social Services: Developing a Policy on Child Sexual Abuse, **Boushel & Noakes.** Developing a Feminist School Policy on Child Sexual Abuse, **O'Hara.** 'Putting Ideas into their Heads': Advising the Young, **Mills.** Child Sexual Abuse Crisis Lines: Advice for Our British Readers.

29 Abortion: the international agenda
Whatever Happened to 'A Woman's Right to Choose'?, **Berer.** More than 'A Woman's Right to Choose'?, **Himmelweit.** Abortion in the Republic of Ireland, **Barry.** Across the Water, **Irish Women's Abortion Support Group.** Spanish Women and the Alton Bill, **Spanish Women's Abortion Support Group.** The Politics of Abortion in Australia: Freedom, Church and State, **Coleman.** Abortion in Hungary, **Szalai.** Women and Population Control in China: Issues of Sexuality, Power and Control, **Hillier.** The Politics of Abortion in Nicaragua: Revolutionary Pragmatism – or Feminism in the realm of necessity?, **Molyneux.** Who Will Sing for Theresa?, **Bernstein.** She's Gotta Have It: The Representation of Black Female Sexuality on Film, **Simmonds.** Poems, **Gallagher.** Dyketactics for Difficult Times: A Review of the 'Homosexuality, Which Homosexuality?' Conference, **Franklin & Stacey.**

30 Capital, gender and skill
Women Homeworkers in Rural Spain, **Lever.** Fact and Fiction: George Egerton and Nellie Shaw, **Butler.** Feminist Political Organization in Iceland: Some Reflections on the Experience of Kwenna Frambothid, **Dominelli & Jonsdottir.**

Under Western Eyes: Feminist Scholarship and Colonial Discourses, **Talpade Mohanty**. Bedroom Horror: The Fatal Attraction of *Intercourse*, **Merck**. AIDS: Lessons from the Gay Community, **Patton**. Poems, **Agbabi**.

31 The past before us: 20 years of feminism

Slow Change or No Change?: Feminism, Socialism and the Problem of Men, **Segal**. There's No Place Like Home: On the Place of Identity in Feminist Politics, **Adams**. New Alliances: Socialist-Feminism in the Eighties, **Harriss**. Other Kinds of Dreams, **Parmar**. Complexity, Activism, Optimism: **Interview with Angela Y. Davis**. To Be or Not To Be: The Dilemmas of Mothering, **Rowbotham**. Seizing Time and Making New: Feminist Criticism, Politics and Contemporary Feminist Fiction, **Lauret**. Lessons from the Women's Movement in Europe, **Haug**. Women in Management, **Coyle**. Sex in the Summer of '88, **Ardill & O'Sullivan**. Younger Women and Feminism, **Hobsbawm & Macpherson**. Older Women and Feminism, **Stacey; Curtis; Summerskill**.

32

'Those Who Die for Life Cannot Be Called Dead': Women and Human Rights Protest in Latin America, **Schirmer**. Violence Against Black Women: Gender, Race and State Responses, **Mama**. Sex and Race in the Labour Market, **Breugel**. The 'Dark Continent': Africa as Female Body in Haggard's Adventure Fiction, **Stott**. Gender, Class and the Welfare State: The Case of Income Security in Australia, **Shaver**. Ethnic Feminism: Beyond the Pseudo-Pluralists, **Gorelick**.

33

Restructuring the Woman Question: *Perestroika* and Prostitution, **Waters**. Contemporary Indian Feminism, **Kumar**. 'A Bit On the Side'?: Gender Struggles in South Africa, **Beall, Hassim and Todes**. 'Young Bess': Historical Novels and Growing Up, **Light**. Madeline Pelletier (1874–1939): The Politics of Sexual Oppression, **Mitchell**.

34 Perverse politics: lesbian issues

Pat Parker: A tribute, **Brimstone**. International Lesbianism: Letter from São Paulo, **Rodrigues**; Israel, **Pittsburgh**, Italy, **Fiocchetto**. The De-eroticization of Women's Liberation: Social Purity Movements and the Revolutionary Feminism of Sheila Jeffreys, **Hunt**. Talking About It: Homophobia in the Black Community, **Gomez & Smith**. Lesbianism and the Labour Party, **Tobin**. Skirting the Issue: Lesbian fashion for the 1990s, **Blackman & Perry**. Butch/Femme Obsessions, **Ardill & O'Sullivan**. Archives: The Will to Remember, **Nestle**; International Archives, **Read**. Audre Lorde: Vignettes and Mental Conversations, **Lewis**. Lesbian Tradition, **Field**. Mapping: Lesbians, AIDS and Sexuality: An interview with Cindy Patton, **O'Sullivan**. Significant Others: Lesbians and Psychoanalytic Theory, **Hamer**. The Pleasure Threshold: Looking at Lesbian Pornography on Film, **Smyth**. Cartoon, **Charlesworth**. Voyages of the Valkyries: Recent Lesbian Pornographic Writing, **Dunn**.

35

Campaign Against Pornography, **Norden**. The Mothers' Manifesto and Disputes over 'Mutterlichkeit', **Chamberlayne**. Multiple Mediations: Feminist Scholarship in the Age of Multi-National Reception, **Mani**. Cagney and

Lacey Revisited, **Alcock & Robson**. Cutting a Dash: The Dress of Radclyffe Hall and Una Troubridge, **Rolley**. Deviant Dress, **Wilson**. The House that Jill Built: Lesbian Feminist Organizing in Toronto, 1976–1980, **Ross**. Women in Professional Engineering: the Interaction of Gendered Structures and Values, **Carter & Kirkup**. Identity Politics and the Hierarchy of Oppression, **Briskin**. Poetry: **Bufkin, Zumwalt**.

36 'The Trouble Is It's Ahistorical': The Problem of the Unconscious in Modern Feminist Theory, **Minsky**. Feminism and Pornography, **Ellis, O'Dair Tallmer**. Who Watches the Watchwomen? Feminists Against Censorship, **Rodgerson & Semple**. Pornography and Violence: What the 'Experts' Really Say, **Segal**. The Woman In My Life: Photography of Women, **Nava**. Splintered Sisterhood: Antiracism in a Young Women's Project, **Connolly**. Woman, Native, Other, **Parmar** interviews **Trinh T. Minh-ha**. Out But Not Down: Lesbians' Experience of Housing, **Edgerton**. Poems: **Evans Davies, Toth, Weinbaum**. Oxford Twenty Years On: Where Are We Now?, **Gamman & O'Neill**. The Embodiment of Ugliness and the Logic of Love: The Danish Redstockings Movement, **Walter**.

37 Theme issue: women, religion and dissent
Black Women, Sexism and Racism: Black or Antiracist Feminism?, **Tang Nain**. Nursing Histories: Reviving Life in Abandoned Selves, **McMahon**. The Quest for National Identity: Women, Islam and the State in Bangladesh, **Kabeer**. Born Again Moon: Fundamentalism in Christianity and the Feminist Spirituality Movement, **McCrickard**. Washing our Linen: One Year of Women Against Fundamentalism, **Connolly**. **Siddiqui** on *Letter to Christendom*, **Bard** on *Generations of Memories*, **Patel** on *Women Living Under Muslim Laws Dossiers 1–6*, Poem, **Kay**. More Cagney and Lacey, **Gamman**.

38 The Modernist Style of Susan Sontag, **McRobbie**. Tantalizing Glimpses of Stolen Glances: Lesbians Take Photographs, **Fraser and Boffin**. Reflections on the Women's Movement in Trinidad, **Mohammed**. Fashion, Representation and Femininity, **Evans & Thornton**. The European Women's Lobby, **Hoskyns**. Hendessi on *Law of Desire: Temporary Marriage in Iran*, **Kaveney** on *Mercy*.

39 Shifting territories: feminism & Europe
Between Hope and Helplessness: Women in the GDR, **Dolling**. Where Have All the Women Gone? Women and the Women's Movement in East Central Europe, **Einhorn**. The End of Socialism in Europe – A New Challenge For Socialist Feminism? **Haug**. The Second 'No': Women in Hungary, **Kiss**. The Citizenship Debate: Women, the State and Ethnic Processes, **Yuval-Davis**. Fortress Europe and Migrant Women, **Morokvasíc**. Racial Equality and 1992, **Dummett**. Questioning *Perestroika*: A Socialist Feminist Interrogation, **Pearson**. Postmodernism and its Discontents, **Soper**. Feminists and Socialism: After the Cold War, **Kaldor**. Socialism Out of the Common Pots, **Mitter**. 1989 and All That, **Campbell**. In Listening Mode, **Cockburn**. **Women in Action: Country by Country**: The Soviet Union; Yugoslavia; Czechoslovakia; Hungary; Poland. **Reports**: International Gay and Lesbian Association: Black Women and Europe 1992.

40 Fleurs du Mal or Second-Hand Roses?: Nathalie Barney, Romaine Brooks, and the 'Originality of the Avant-Garde', **Elliott & Wallace**. Poem, **Tyler-Bennett**. Feminism and Motherhood: An American 'Reading, **Snitow**. Qualitative Research, Appropriation of the 'Other' and Empowerment, **Opie**. Disabled Women and the Feminist Agenda, **Begum**. Postcard From the Edge: Thoughts on the 'Feminist Theory: An International Debate' Conference at Glasgow University, July 1991, **Radstone**. Review Essay, **Munt**.

41 Editorial. The Selling of HRT: Playing on the Fear Factor, **Worcester & Whatley**. The Cancer Drawings of Catherine Arthur, **Sebastyen**. Ten Years of Women's Health 1982–92, **James**. AIDS Activism: Women and AIDS Activism in Victoria, Australia, **Mitchell**. A Woman's Subject, **Friedli**. HIV and the Invisibility of Women: Is there a Need to Redefine AIDS?, **Scharf & Toole**. Lesbians Evolving Health Care: Cancer and AIDS, **Winnow**. Now is the Time for Feminist Criticism: A Review of *Asinimali!*, **Steinberg**. Ibu or the Beast: Gender Interests in Two Indonesian Women's Organizations, **Wieringa**. Reports on Motherlands: Symposium on African, Carribean and Asian Women's Writing, **Smart**. The European Forum of Socialist Feminists, **Bruegel**. Review Essay, **Gamman**.

42 Feminist fictions
Editorial. Angela Carter's *The Bloody Chamber* and the Decolonization of Feminine Sexuality, **Makinen**. Feminist Writing: Working with Women's Experience, **Haug**. Three Aspects of Sex in Marge Piercy's *Fly Away Home*, **Hauser**. Are They Reading Us? Feminist Teenage Fiction, **Bard**. Sexuality in Lesbian Romance Fiction, **Hermes**. A Psychoanalytic Account for Lesbianism, **Castendyk**. Mary Wollstonecraft and the Problematic of Slavery, **Ferguson**. Reviews.

43 Issues for feminism
Family, Motherhood and Zulu Nationalism: The Politics of the Inkatha Women's Brigade, **Hassim**. Postcolonial Feminism and the Veil: Thinking the Difference, **Abu Odeh**. Feminism, the Menopause and Hormone Replacement Therapy, **Lewis**. Feminism and Disability, **Morris**. 'What is Pornography?': An Analysis of the Policy Statement of the Campaign Against Pornography and Censorship, **Smith**. Reviews.

44 Nationalisms and national identities
Women, Nationalism and Islam in Contemporary Political Discourse in Iran, **Yeganeh**. Feminism, Citizenship and National Identity, **Curthoys**. Remapping and Renaming: New Cartographies of Identity, Gender and Landscape in Ireland, **Nash**. Rap Poem: Easter 1991, **Medbh**. Family Feuds: Gender, Nationalism and the Family, **McClintock**. Women as Activists; Women as Symbols: A Study of the Indian Nationalist Movement, **Thapar**. Gender, Nationalisms and National Identities: Bellagio Symposium Report, **Hall**. Culture or Citizenship? Notes from the Gender and Colonialism Conference, Galway, Ireland, May 1992, **Connolly**. Reviews.

45 Thinking through ethnicities

Audre Lorde: Reflections. Re-framing Europe: Engendered Racisms, Ethnicities and Nationalisms in Contemporary Western Europe, **Brah**. Towards a Multicultural Europe? 'Race' Nation and Identity in 1992 and Beyond, **Bhavnani**. Another View: Photo Essay, **Pollard**. Growing Up White: Feminism, Racism and the Social Geography of Childhood, **Frankenberg**. Poem, **Kay**. Looking Beyond the Violent Break-up of Yugoslavia, **Coulson**. Personal Reactions of a Bosnian Woman to the War in Bosnia, **Harper**. Serbian Nationalism: Nationalism of My Own People, **Korac**. Belgrade Feminists 1992: Separation, Guilt and Identity Crisis, **Mladjenovic, Litricin**. Report on a Council of Europe Minority Youth Committee Seminar on Sexism and Racism in Western Europe, **Walker**. Reviews.

46 Sexualities: challenge and change

Chips, Coke and Rock-'n-Roll: Children's Mediation of an Invitation to a First Dance Party, **Rossiter**. Power and Desire: The Embodiment of Female Sexuality, **Holland, Ramazanoglu, Sharpe, Thomson**. Two Poems, **Janzen**. A Girton Girl on the Throne: Queen Christina and Versions of Lesbianism 1906–1933. Changing Interpretations of the Sexuality of Queen Christina of Sweden, **Waters**. The Pervert's Progress: An Analysis of 'The Story of O' and The Beauty Trilogy, **Ziv**. Dis-Graceful Images: Della Grace and Lesbian Sadomasochism, **Lewis**. Reviews.

47

Virgin Territories and Motherlands: Colonial and Nationalist Representations of Africa, **Innes**. The Impact of the Islamic Movement in Egypt, **Shukrallah**. Mothering on the Lam: Politics, Gender Fantasies and Maternal Thinking in Women Associated with Armed, Clandestine Organizations in the US, **Zwerman**. Treading the Traces of Discarded History: Photo-Essay, **Marchant**. The Feminist Production of Knowledge: Is Deconstruction a Practice for Women?, **Nash**. 'Divided We Stand': Sex, Gender and Sexual Difference, **Moore**. Reviews.

48 Sex and the state

Editorial. Legislating Sexuality in the Post-Colonial State, **Alexander**. State, Family and Personal Responsibility: The Changing Balance for Lone Mothers in the United Kingdom, **Millar**. Moral Rhetoric and Public Health Pragmatism: The Recent Politics of Sex Education, **Thomson**. Through the Parliamentary Looking Glass: 'Real' and 'Pretend' Families in Contemporary British Politics, **Reinhold**. In Search of Gender Justice: Sexual Assault and the Criminal Justice System, **Gregory and Lees**. God's Bullies: Attacks on Abortion, **Hadley**. Sex, Work, HIV and the State – an interview with Nel Druce, **Overs**. Reviews.

49 Feminist politics – Colonial/postcolonial worlds

Women on the March: Right-Wing Mobilization in Contemporary India, **Mazumdar**. Colonial Encounters in Late-Victorian England: Pandita Ramabai at Cheltenham and Wantage, **Burton**. Subversive Intent: A Social theory of Gender, **Maharaj**. My Discourse/My Self: Therapy as Possibility (for women who eat compulsively), **Hopwood**. Poems, **Donohue**. Review Essays. Reviews.

D U K E
UNIVERSITY PRESS

Fatal Advice
How Safe-Sex Education
Went Wrong
Cindy Patton
"A book of life and death importance
on the politics of safe-sex. I can think
of few other books that contribute so
significantly to both cultural criticism
and, in every sense of the term, public
health."—Constance Penley
Series Q
200 pages, 10 illus., £14.95 paper

Man-Made Medicine
Women's Health, Public Policy,
and Reform
Kary L. Moss, editor
"This unique anthology fills a void in
the literature of public health policy.
It provides a prism for understanding
how women's well-being is affected
by hidden assumptions about color,
class, and culture. Destined to become
a classic . . . "—Patricia Williams,
Professor of Law, Columbia University
304 pages, £14.95 paper

Gaze and Voice as
Love Objects
SIC 1
Renata Salecl and Slavoj Žižek, editors
"A marvelous collection of essays written
by some of the most prominent figures
working today from within a Lacanian
paradigm."—John Mowitt
SIC
304pp, 9 b&w photos, £15.95 pb

Arrogant Beggar
Anzia Yezierska
Introduction by Katherine Stubbs
186 pages, £11.95 paper

Sex Scandal
The Private Parts of Victorian Fiction
William A. Cohen
Never has the Victorian novel appeared
so perverse as it does in these pages—
and never has its perversity seemed so
fundamental to its accomplishments.
Series Q
272 pages, £15.95 paper

Questions of Travel
Postmodern Discourses
of Displacement
Caren Kaplan
Explores the various metaphoric uses
of travel and displacement in literary
and feminist theory,
Post-Contemporary Interventions
256 pages, £15.95 paper

Passing and the Fictions
of Identity
Elaine K. Ginsberg, editor
The essays in this volume consider a
wide range of texts and moments that
raise significant questions about the
political motivations inherent in the
origins and maintenance of identity
categories and boundaries.
New Americanists
296 pages, 6 illus., £15.95 paper

Nothing Happens
Chantal Akerman's Hyperrealist
Everyday
Ivone Margulies
Presents the first comprehensive study
of Chantal Akerman, who has gained a
reputation as one of the most significant
filmmakers working today.
280 pages, 26 b&w photos, £15.95 paper

c/o AUPG, 1 Gower Street
London WC1E 6HA
Tel/Fax: (0171) 580 3994/5
email: monk@easynet.co.uk

Budapest Diary
In Search of the Motherbook
SUSAN RUBIN SULEIMAN
"Pensive, forthright journal. . . . cultural reportage and astute political observation enrich her intimate story."—*Booklist*
£23.95 hb

Rue Ordener, Rue Labat
SARAH KOFMAN
Translated by Ann Smock
"Describes the horrors that [Kofman] and her family endured in Paris during the German occupation . . . short, gripping memoir, adeptly translated."
—*Library Journal*
£9.50 pb, £23.95 hb

Searching for Saleem
An Afghan Woman's Odyssey
FAROOKA GAUHARI
Foreword by Nancy Dupree
A first-person account of a national tragedy that interrupted daily life in Afghanistan after the communist coup of April 1978.
£32.95 hb

Covered Wagon Women, Volume 2
Covered Wagon Women, Volume 3
EDITED AND COMPILED BY
KENNETH L. HOLMES
£12 pb each volume

Underground River and Other Stories
INÉS ARREDONDO
Translated by Cynthia Steele
Foreword by Elena Poniatowska
Twelve haunting stories by one of Mexico's greatest women writers.
£11 pb/£23.95 hb

Nevermore
MARIE REDONNET
Translated with an introduction by Jordan Stump
"A frenetic erotic thriller, . . . a chilling portrait of mankind's vulgarity and duplicity."—*Times Literary Supplement*
£11 pb/£29.95 hb

Slander
LINDA LÊ
Translated with an afterword by Esther Allen
Like author Linda Lê, the young narrator of this novel is from Vietnam and is a writer, a "dirty foreigner writing in French." Her story reveals three generations of a cursed family.
£13 pb/£28.50 hb

Conversations with Maryse Condé
FRANÇOISE PFAFF
An exploration of the life and art of Maryse Condé.
£14 pb/£32.95 hb

Automatic Woman
The Representation of Woman in Surrealism
KATHARINE CONLEY
Through insightful analyses of works by a range of writers and artists, Conley develops a complex view of Surrealist portrayals of Woman.
£32.95 hb

Women in German Yearbook 11
EDITED BY SARA FRIEDRICHSMEYER AND PATRICIA HERMINGHOUSE
£17 pb/£35 hb

University of Nebraska Press
c/o Academic & University Publishers Group · 1 Gower St. London WC1E 6HA

MA in Gender Studies

This new, interdisciplinary course is based in the Departments of Government, History, Literature and Sociology and may be taken full- or part-time.

Content: 20-week interdisciplinary core course, dissertation and two 20-week options or their equivalent. Specific options available vary from year to year but presently include:

Articulations of Power: Race, Class and Gender; Feminism and Politics; Formations of Masculinity; Gender and Work; Gender in Early Modern Europe 1500 - 1700; Language and Identity; Psychoanalysis and Art Theory; Women Writing

Teaching team: Enam Al-Wer, Andrew Canessa, Leaonore Davidoff, Anthony Fletcher, Miriam Glucksman, Catherine Hall, Margaret Iversen, Elaine Jordan, Aletta Norval, Vicky Randall, Michael Roper, Alison Rowlands.

For further information, please contact: Linda Day, Department of Government, University of Essex, Wivenhoe Park, Colchester CO4 3SQ. Telephone: 01206 872751. E-mail: lindad@essex.ac.uk

Promoting excellence in research, scholarship and education

 University of Essex